I have seen par
people wouldn'

I have seen stratus clouds on
fire off the shoulder of Fuji.

I have watched rainbows
glitter in the dawn near the
Severn Bridge gate.

But all those moments will be
lost in time, like sweat in rain.

Time to live.

by Tim Gardiner

Great Britain Aquathlon Team Captain Yiannis Christodoulou on the parkrun bug:

"It all began with parkrun which opened me up to the world of running. Parkrun helped me get active without the pressure of a race. It allows people to be active and introduces them to running and from there you never know how far you can go."

Yiannis has certainly achieved plenty in the world of athletics after he starting running in 2012. He was 2019 European and National Aquathlon Champion (Age Group) and is competing in the 2020 European Triathlon Championships. Yiannis continues to inspire all of us that turn up on a Saturday with nothing but hope that we may complete the hallowed 3.1 miles in a quicker time than last week.

GLADE RUNNER
by Tim Gardiner

by Tim Gardiner

First published in the UK in 2020 by Stour Valley Publishing

A CIP Catalogue Record of this book is available from the British Library

ISBN: 978-1-913450-02-1 (PB)

Printed & Bound by Mixam UK Ltd, Watford, UK

Stour Valley Publishing
3 Tiberius Close
Haverhill
CB9 0NP
www.stourvalleypublishing.co.uk

FOREWORD

Tim's poetic journey follows in the footsteps of prolific parkrun tourists. To be a parkrun tourist, you only need to visit a parkrun that is not your home event. It really is that simple. This may be one down the road or a parkrun in some far flung corner of parkrunworld, many miles from home. Touring parkrunworld is like being given a free passport to discover (mostly) green spaces across the world that you may otherwise never have heard of. The incredible global growth of parkrun is testament to the success of the movement.

Levels of parkrun tourism will vary depending on who you talk to. Some like to get their parkrun fix when visiting friends and relatives, many, while working away from home or on holiday (if you're lucky enough to be in a parkrun country). For others, parkrun tourism has become a game, a bit of fun added to their parkrunday, whilst for some, parkrun tourism has become an obsession. There are a few who run their first 50 or 100 parkruns each at a different venue, exploring parkrunworld as they go and never really having a home parkrun (despite being required to select one when they registered). Some even run a parkrun in every parkrun country, or run at over 250 different events. Both the parkrun show and our current podcast (with me now) delight in tales from parkrun tourists across the world.

The introduction of the Running Challenges extension has fuelled the desire of many parkrunners to achieve goals they never imagined when they began their parkrun journey. As parkrun grows, so do the lengths that people will go to, using parkrun to write their adventures. The beauty of doing so is being able to tap into communities of an extended parkrun family along the way. Meeting like-minded people across the world, and being fully accepted as part of their community is magical. It was amazing for my daughter and I to experience this on our parkrun trip to...

Australia, New Zealand and Singapore. The world of parkrun is incrementally rebuilding a community spirit that has been fractured by modern lifestyles, and not just locally, the incredible thing about this community is that it is global. Tim's poetry tour of 50 events captures the individual community spirit of each parkrun, many of which I have run with my daughter.

Happy parkrunning

Nicola Forwood A8863

INTRODUCTION

My parkrun journey began at Great Notley in Essex on 7th October 2017.

Cajoled into it by a work colleague, I made the classic beginner's mistake of haring around the first lap, before the hill did its worse. My colleague thought I was having a heart attack as she destroyed me in the sprint finish. It was clear that I wasn't very fit at all, trailing in at a very modest 35:51. But my parkrun journey had begun and as the weeks passed, the finish times started to drop towards the magical 30 minute mark. On my eighth run, at Kesgrave in Ipswich, I recorded the first sub-30 (28:53). Spurred on, the times continued to fall until my current personal best of 25:12 was attained at Norwich, Norfolk, in December 2019. I'd lost 15 kilos in weight on this journey, the main reason for commencing running in 2017. Running over 1000 miles in parkruns and training has also helped to improve my mental health, specifically the highs and lows of bipolar.

I'd also started touring different venues with an aim to first reach the UK Most Events Table (20 events). The parkrun poetry also began to flow with poems for run reports as far apart as Mersea Island (Essex) and Moors Valley (Dorset). The first run report I was let loose on was for the newly established parkrun at Sloughbottom in Norwich, followed the next week by Loch Neaton in Breckland. The parkrun bug had really bitten, the aim to reach 50 events sometime in 2020.

Results have been mixed to say the least. My highest parkrun finish of 13th came out of a small field of runners at Haverhill. I've made the top 50 on 15 occasions, a modest achievement, as is my average run time of 27:55 and age grade around 50%. Parkrunning has led to other low key athletic achievements: a top 10 finish occurring in the Witch Finder Trail 5 km in Mistley, Essex, in 2019. Twice (2017, 2018), I've come second in the Great Yarmouth Road Runners' Yuletide Doubles race in Waveney Forest, Norfolk.

Along the way, I became acquainted with the wonders of parkrun tourist challenges. The Pirates (run seven Cs and an R), Stayin' Alive (run three Bs and three Gs), in addition to the traditional Christmas Day parkrun and the New Year's Day Double (two runs in a day!). Plus there's the addiction of a tourist streak of consecutive different events (my record is 41). The logistics of getting around to a different run every week becomes progressively more complicated and eventually life got in the way for me. But tourism is fun and gives you a chance to meet new people and challenge yourself over different terrains. The hills of Sheringham for instance are a lung busting delight!

I'm currently trying to run every parkrun course in East Anglia (Cambs, Norfolk and Suffolk); a feat I'm calling East Ran-glia (38 events)! I'm 27 parkruns to the good, well on the way to completing Tour-folk (16/17 events), Suff-ok ticked off (11/11), but some distance from tucking into the Camb-which (2/10)! I've travelled around 25000 km to complete the 50 parkruns, the majority of this (18000 km) being accounted for by a trip to Japan (not just for a parkrun I must add).

A knee injury during late 2019, saw me turn to power walking during the recovery. Power walking as my parkrun alter ego, Mike 'The Shape' Myers, in overalls and white mask, I completed several parkruns, achieving a personal best of 40:28 during a Halloween fancy dress event at King's Lynn. The pace of 13 minutes/mile compares to 8 minutes/mile for my fastest running parkrun. Power walking at the back of the field is an interesting experience, allowing you to chat and connect with more athletes. Having said this, walking as quickly as possible is an out of breath experience and training is required to obtain lower times. I found being in character as power walking, fictional psychopath Michael Myers from the classic horror film Halloween, a useful aid to maintaining the relentless, mechanical march for 3.1 miles.

The aim of this book is to document, through poetry and prose, the 50 different events I've run in the order that I first visited them from December 2018 onwards. The text includes haiku (short, 3 line poems from Japan), tanka (5 line poems, also Japanese), haibun (haiku with prose), and also a limerick and free verse poems. Cheekily, I've reworked famous poems (e.g. John Donne) to give them a parkrun flavour where they have a tenuous link to the event in question. Perhaps even less respectful are the tweaks made to Glen Campbell's hit Galveston to make it relevant to Gorleston parkrun. I hope you enjoy this poetic tour of the parkruns of the east and beyond.

Tim Gardiner, 2020

CONTENTS

Border crossings

1. HARWICH

The windswept promenade of the Essex coastal town of Harwich, makes for a pleasant parkrun. The sight of Queen Victoria on the cliff-top, then the High Light Tower on the shore reminds runners of Harwich's Victorian past, before a row of beach huts precedes the half-way turnaround. The final dash up the slope takes a little edge off any speed that may have been accrued, but it's still a fast course as long as it's not windy. On a summer day, it's worth exploring a little after parkrun. The two lighthouses in the old town have an interesting history. The High Lighthouse and Low Lighthouse worked as 'leading lights' guiding ships into the harbour until shifting sands rendered them obsolete when a new channel formed.

My favourite memory of Harwich parkrun is running it with my son Joseph and Helen Ivory. It was the early days of running for me and Joseph and we struggled in the last mile having gone out too quickly. There was a wonderful three-way Mexican sprint at the end, which Joseph with his younger legs inevitably won.

time lord...
clicking the stopwatch
he reminisces

three runners
approach the funnel...
Mexican stand-off

2. MERSEA ISLAND

This parkrun has the distinction of being on a large island off the Essex coast. You have to cross the Strood, a causeway where the road can be flooded by high tides if you're unlucky. Mersea Island also has a population of red squirrels, a rare mammal in the UK. The introduced squirrels are doing well in their new home. One may be spotted along the parkrun course one day! To commemorate the end of World War I, in 2018 wooden soldiers were placed along the salt marsh, a moving memorial for those who fought and died. Runners also pass by a pillbox and through two wooded sections, which can be slippery in wet weather. The views of the Colne Estuary are stunning, from the two and a half lap course.

pillbox in the wood
a young runner
sprints past us
along the seawall
unknown once more

seawall soldiers
water runs through
the marsh creek

corner cutter
a red squirrel strays
from the path

downhill dash
dad says 'bomb it'
then falls over

3. KESGRAVE

I've run Kesgrave a few times and it's a quick dash round a football field, along a green lane, before the switchback which leads to my favourite woodland part of the course near the finish. On one occasion, a storm necessitated a change of route, much to the annoyance of my son who had psyched himself up for the bumpy woodland sprint at the end. Safety must come first though, and we enjoyed an extremely hard run into the gale!

the car left
r u n   n   i   n   g
personal best

last minute
route change....
pbs stay the same

age grade
some things get better
with time

4. GORLESTON CLIFFS

In the town where I grew up, the parkrun takes you on a tour of Gorleston Cliffs with some majestic views of the beach and coastline towards Hopton. If you get there early enough, the sunrise will be your reward, while in winter, cormorants often fly overhead on their way to Scroby Sands. The course is two laps, starting on the cliff top and finishing on the lower promenade. An assortment of Great Yarmouth Road Runners and Bungay Black Dogs are usually on display, as well as old school friends and my geography teacher who is much faster and older than me!

fistful of tokens...
a parkrun marshal
quick on the draw

record attendance
the runner jumps
over a spaniel

half a parkrun
my sick son eats
a full English

geography teacher
his route to the finish
mapped out

Jack o' lantern
a boy carves his way
through the field

fastest split
Deirdre tears through
palm leaves

Run Report: Gorleston, Oh, Gorleston! #544

Ten years ago a parkrun was started on Gorleston Cliffs by a small band of enthusiastic volunteers led by local running stalwart, Chris Harbord. Supported by volunteer coordinator, Jim Spong, the parkrun has blossomed with 36 amazing volunteers for event 544. It was the 12th parkrun in the country (and first in the eastern region) after Bushy kicked things off in 2004. To mark 15 years of parkrun this morning (number 544), we were joined by Andrew Lane, one of Paul Sinton-Hewitt's 13 disciples on that momentous October morning in Bushy Park.

The first Gorleston Cliffs parkrun on 25th April 2009 was attended by just 10 people, three of whom, Peter Smith, Peter John Westgate and Janet Sanderson (an incredible 406 runs at Gorleston), ran this morning. They were an integral part of the mass of 367 athletes today, illustrating how much the parkrun has grown since 2009. I decided to walk this morning due to a dodgy knee, and was overtaken near Jay Jay's on lap one by Ian 'Try-Run-Osaur' Henderson, running well despite the wind jostling his costume. Life at the back of the field can be a bit lonely, but I was accompanied by visually-impaired runner, Sarah Wilby, and her guide, Laura Latimer, for the second lap. Congratulations to both on a solid run, managing to escape the relentless march of Mike 'The Shape' Myers in the final dash to the line.

At the front, Tyler Bilyard ran a lightning 16:23 as the first male finisher, while Allyna Mukuya (J11-14) blitzed the field to be first female finisher with 20:33. Milestones were plentiful: Mei-Ann Stevens (Junior 10), Meryn Payne and Dee Townsend (50), and my old school mate, Jamie Mordecai (100). Congratulations to them all.

And finally, I leave you with Glen Campbell's classic hit, reworked for Gorleston Cliffs:

Gorleston, oh, Gorleston,
I still hear your seawinds blowing;
I still see her Garmin glowing.
She was twenty mins, when I left Gorleston.
Gorleston, oh, Gorleston,
I still hear your seawaves crashin',
while I watch the camera flashin'.
I clean my phone, and dream of Gorleston.
I still see her running by
the water,
Jogging there looking out to sea.
And is she warming up for me,
On the beach where we used to run?
Gorleston, oh!
Gorleston, I am so afraid of walking,
Before I dry the tears she's running,
Before I watch your sea birds flying in the sun,
at Gorleston, at Gorleston

5. LOWESTOFT

I took my son to Lowestoft for the parkrun before Christmas 2018. I donned an elf t-shirt and hat, my son decided to go for the conventional Santa hat. It was a chilly but dry morning, as we set off along the prom, running past the beach huts before the first ascent of the infamous CEFAS Hill. The second climb is a demoralising but mercifully short run up the slope, before the wonderful downhill sprint to the finish. But be careful not to overdo the speed or you could hit the wall!

CEFAS Hill
a slippery slope
to the finish

overtaken
cloud shadows
on the prom

ignoring the
marshal
a runner hits
the wall

6. NORWICH

My first visit to Norwich was on Christmas Day, 2018. It was a frosty morning in Eaton Park and the paths were skiddy. Over 1100 athletes turned up, including plenty of fancy dress elves and an impressive dinosaur. One of the largest parkrun attendances, there was a lot of jostling for position at the start, but it was a joyous occasion. It's also worth a look in the pond to see if the parkrun's most faithful supporter is around.

before the run
the heron
stretches
a shadow

Haibun:

Negative Split to Norwich

As I sprint across Breydon Bridge, the 8.15 is just leaving Vauxhall. The first mile is easy, the Acle Straight clear of traffic on a Saturday morning. In the wing mirror there's no sign of the train, perhaps it's on the way to Berney Arms instead. The windmill at the halfway point marks a kink in the Roman-like road, my pace slowing a little.

double-take
in the rear-view mirror
single carriage

Hard on our shoulder, the pursuer is relentless, only a mile to go to the Acle Roundabout. I lean on the accelerator, the road ahead of me is empty. A tractor pulls out of a field, the air turns blue within the car. Alongside us now, it's all over.

first finisher
a second-hand Nissan
good for age

7. MALDON PROM

Run Report: Lord of the wings! #323

On a rainy October morning, 266 athletes descended on Prom Park for a bracing parkrun. It was World Migratory Bird Day, a very fitting occasion as the parkrun loops around the statue of Byrhtnoth (try spelling his name after a few drinks!). Here runners and walkers gain majestic views of the mudflats and salt marsh of the Blackwater Estuary and Northey Island, teeming with overwintering birds such as curlew, godwit and redshank. On my last run at Maldon, a flock of lapwings passed above us at the statue, a truly awe-inspiring sight which led me to write this short poem:

lapwing flock
over Byrhtnoth
the display flight
of a tailwalker
on the prom

The title of this report is partly inspired by J.R.R. Tolkien who, in addition to writing The Hobbit and The Lord of the Rings trilogy, studied the famous Battle of Maldon poem about good old Byrhtnoth and even wrote a follow up poem. This is of course supplementary reading for any hard-core Maldon parkrunner and of scant use when going for a personal best. As my son frequently says, my run reports have very little to do with running! But for a poet, a horde of orcs rampaging around the course is too good a metaphor to resist! Another migratory bird to look out for is the inspiration behind this short poem:

> the dark belly
> of a brent goose
> rises from the creek
> like a balrog shadow
> without flames

But without further ado, the parkrun itself! Nikki Hills (21:59) and Aaron Graves (18:00) excelled as first finishers. Despite the rain, 36 personal bests were achieved; congratulations to all. This week, 126 athletes beat the poet (27:49), a sorry state of affairs for the waffling wordsmith on his way back from injury. Last time I was here (December 2018), my son managed to lose his jumper! It wasn't handed in, so good tidings to whoever ended up with an extra Christmas present.....

> 'twas the run
> after Christmas
> when all along the prom
> not a jumper was stirring
> except my blue one!

This desecration of Clement Clarke Moore's classic poem, leads nicely on to the Santa marshals that we had today who are involved in organising the Santa Fun Run at Great Notley Country Park on 15th December, raising money for Hope House, a charity aiming to break the cycle of homelessness. I couldn't resist a cheeky "Ho – Ho – Ho" in the style of Alan Rickman as thanks! Well, we did "come out to the coast, get together, have a few laughs!"

We also had several runners from Young Minds, whose aim is to help young people with mental health problems. Check out #HelloYellow on twitter. The event was well supported by 21 fantastic volunteers. Lastly, I must thank run director Sue Smith, for inviting me to write this run report.

Run Report: Hitchcock Presents #327

On the 30th anniversary of the fall of the Berlin Wall, 301 athletes assembled in the spirit of parkrun togetherness for this remembrance weekend. At a time when the world appears more divided than ever, it's heartening that a common goal can bring people closer. We should never forget the price of division.

On a lighter note, it's lovely when you're allowed to write a second report for a parkrun. This one is just as tenuous as the last (Lord of the Wings #323) in its link to running. Firstly, I must explain the title. Last week I speed walked King's Lynn parkrun dressed as everyone's favourite fictional psychopath, Michael Myers, from the 1978 film Halloween. The movie was inspired by Alfred Hitchcock's 1960 classic, Psycho. Interestingly, we had two Hitchcocks take part in the Halloween run at King's Lynn! So what does this have to do with Maldon, I don't hear you ask? Well very little, except that Hitchcock possibly drew inspiration for his suspense films from a visit to Maldon District. The Birds is certainly an apt film for Prom Park and the surrounding mudflats and salt marshes which teem with avian life. The following run report has a series of 3 line Hitchcock haiku (or Hitchku), each reflecting a part of the course, including the title of one of his films!

Dial P for parkrun

As usual I was late for the run briefing, just catching a few words from top run director, Elaine Vaughan. Milestones were achieved by Jacqui Smythe and Paul Nolan (50 Club). On a personal note, my son and me got to a combined total of 100 parkruns (Joseph 30 runs, dad 70).

rear window
I can just hear the briefing
from the toilet

I told my son not to go out too quick. I might as well have been talking to the birds for all the notice he takes. But the arm's length rule keeps him close around the off-road meadow section.

psycho
unexpected sprinter
on mud and grass

Emerging from the trees, we thank one of the 21 volunteers. The commotion from our banter causes a lapwing to take flight from the mudflats near the statue. This is my favourite part of the course, the view of Northey Island, breath-taking (as is the running!).

the birds
around Byrhtnoth
a flock of runners

On the first lap, we approach the lake, the dull ache in my knee indicates that the early pace will not last much longer. But still I wave at the marshals and run director atop the escarpment plinth, prominent like a miniature Minas Tirith.

north by northwest
we wind around the lake
with the breeze

By now, the eventual female first finisher, Heidi Steele (19:35), this week's Prom Queen, is nearing the funnel. The pace of the front runners comes as no surprise, the male first finisher, Henry Clarke, running superbly (18:14).

a lady vanishes
around the lake
men fade away

The fly in the ointment for me is always at the end of lap one. I often wonder how much a barkrunner can bring to their owner's time on the precipitous slope next to the grassy escarpment of Minas Tirith!

the 39 steps
a dog drags its owner
up the slope

The second perambulation of the meadow brings its own challenges. Gone is the energy with which I scampered around it on lap one. The run director's words ringing in my ears, I commit the ultimate Maldon Prom doozy to shave a few seconds off my time!

I confess
I cut a corner
in the meadow

I'm running through metaphorical treacle now, but my son has seen an opportunity to push me even harder to deaden dad's legs for the sprint in which he will inevitably emerge victorious. He has given me enough Rope on this run…

vertigo
a gull takes flight
from high railings

The north face is conquered for the last time; the funnel seems like it's farther away than before. Formalities over, barcode and finish Tolkien scanned, I wonder what happened to my son's fleece top all those months ago.

to catch a thief
still no sign
of the jumper

And finally, to go with the 50 pbs, 102 people beat the poet this week (time 26:44, a new course pb!). I wonder if any of them committed the cardinal parkrun sin…

the wrong man
an unknown athlete
takes a token home

And to finish up this tenuously titled run report, Hitchcock's great grandfather was born in Essex (c.1791); the director strongly linked with the village of Dedham, six ancestors having lived there. There's also a Hitchcock's Meadow (it's got orchids and glow-worms!) in nearby Danbury which I assume has nothing to do with the director!

Run Report: World in motion #346

The International Women's Day (IWD) parkrun was a joyous affair. Parkrunners came dressed in purple to celebrate the occasion and run the world (look out for all 10 song titles by female singers). Some days, I just don't know what to do with myself, but Saturday is parkrun time. On this pleasant, sunny morning, 420 athletes (194 women – 46%) listened with respect to run director Alison's briefing, delivered as usual from atop Minas Tirith. This woman's work came to an end, a two-week stint as RD successfully completed.

Tourists were from exotic places like Chelmsford and Manningtree but no-one had been all around the world. Milestones were celebrated including Cole Eardley (10 Club) and new 50 Club members Dave Callow, Joe McEwan and Teresa Mitchell. Mark Gillam completed his 100th parkrun. Walking back to happiness this morning were Ella and Kate Priest on the latter's return from injury. In all there were five priests in attendance, like a prayer we had ecumenical matters covered!

The route was lined with 25 volunteers, 13 of them women including fab volunteer co-ordinator Elaine. Thanks to all of these amazing people. It was a nice change to not have the wind beneath my wings, but a girl on fire was female first finisher Heidi Steele storming round in 19:36 (8th position); this week's Prom Queen. There were also superb runs from Kate Lawson (21:42) and Emily Smith (21:51), the former recording a new pb. Beatrice Long was first Junior Under 11 female finisher completing the course in 29:51, a new pb and highly impressive. Wendy Simpson ran 28:25 (age grade 72:43%) to be the fastest female finisher over 65. Sisters are doin' it for themselves!

In keeping with the IWD theme, 31 women beat the poet (pos. 171: 27:37). I was concerned with pacing my son Joseph on his return from injury, he particularly appreciated RD Alison's words of encouragement from Minas Tirith at the start of the difficult second lap. We were competing in the Vitality Running World Cup 2020 to help Unicef raise money for child vaccination against diseases such as Tuberculosis. Download the app and get running a 5K every week to contribute to your nation's weekly mileage. Currently, South Africa is in first place, while the United Kingdom is third. The top countries in the qualifiers will progress to the last 16 on March 14 and so on. The Final is on April 4, a parkrun day!!!

Register and contribute your parkrun efforts at https://runningworldcup.com

Poetry Corner

In the artistic portion of this week's run report, some very fine haiku poetry from two outstanding international poets. The short haiku poems which follow are very relevant to Prom Park:

Marta Majorka Chocilowska
(Poland)

musing
a cry from the riverside
tears the fog

Published in Blithe Spirit #28.1, 2018

Iliyana Stoyanova
(Bulgaria)

misty lake
only the arch
of a swan's neck

Published in Living Haiku Anthology, 2017

8. BRUNDALL

The first half of my New Year's Day double in 2019, the run commencing at 8.30, allowing runners time to get to their second parkrun of the day. In my case, I'd be off to Catton Park for a 10.30am start.

At Brundall, we had a good turnout of several hundred runners, including many Great Yarmouth Road Runners. The course itself is four laps of the newly planted community woodland with an interesting kink in the middle, and the infamous, uphill slope of the 'travelator' at the end of each one. As usual, there was an interesting assortment of people in attendance.

New Year's Day
long-suffering legs ache
on the travelator

foot surgeon
taking a keen interest
in my distance runs

9. CATTON

The second half of my New Year's Day double in 2019. Catton Park is a fantastic location for a run with open pasture with scattered oaks, but don't be fooled, it's not completely flat. Athletes must ascend the south face of the infamous Catterhorn twice. After the New Year's run, I got speaking to Ian R. Thomas who was the first finisher at the inaugural Gorleston Cliffs parkrun in 2009. He's also finished the Spartathlon (153 miles), a recreation of the famous Marathon to Athens run by Pheidippides in around 490 BC.

Sparta run
I'm out of breath
just talking about it

A scanner went missing when I visited, and caused quite a stir on social media about who finished where. As one of the affected athletes, I wrote this light-hearted tale:

Haibun:

Sad Bob

They say he was never the same after that run. He'd pushed it so hard for a sub 25; the missing scanner simply broke his spirit. Descending into despair Bob gave up running and never returned to Catton Park. Sad Bob died with nothing but his barcode, a promising running career cut short. His ghost is said to run the course every New Year's Day, starting at 10.30 am and finishing 24 minutes 59 seconds later.

moonless night
on White Woman Lane
solace in her arms

10. FRITTON LAKE

Being born in Great Yarmouth and growing up in Gorleston, the pine woods of the Fritton area in East Norfolk were a childhood haunt. The sadly now defunct Fritton Lake parkrun was as close to running on the forest moon of Endor as possible. To the best of my knowledge, I don't think an Ewok-costumed athlete ever ran the parkrun. The next best option for such an enthusiast would be Brandon Country Park. RIP Fritton Lake.

forest moon
out of the undergrowth
a muntjac

Haibun:

The Speeder

Racing between the pines, a hunter in pursuit, I nervously glance over my shoulder. They're not in view yet, my prey unsighted too. As I jump over a rotten log, a startled escapee from Squirrel Hall leaps into the brambles. Thundering downhill, I trip on a tree root but regain balance quickly. It's clear I won't catch my quarry, the Stormtrooper going well despite the humidity of his microclimate. Behind, my stalker is gaining ground, their light footfall obvious to pricked ears. The final turn is made, the slog uphill begins, the chaser a few paces back...

finish line
my son's breath
pips me to the line

11. SIZEWELL

This was a must-visit parkrun on the wind-swept Suffolk coast. My son was a little concerned that the giant golf-ball reactor of Sizewell B nuclear power station might explode. I told him not to worry if it did, we won't be running quick enough to escape! This run is a straight out and back course through the dunes. Near the turnaround point, you get to admire the reedbeds of the RSPB's Minsmere reserve. The run is also started with a nuclear warning siren, how cool is that?

first light
a crab scuttles
across the sand

dune slack
lichens crunch
under our feet

by the dome
gorse flowers
in midwinter

12. MULBARTON

A visit to Mulbarton near Norwich on an icy January morning in 2019 saw athletes run the winter course which is five laps of the football fields. The summer route is around the old common and looks worth a run. They also have a bus which has been converted into a café, which is a welcome post-run refuge. My visit here, saw me run an ill-advised and rare 25 minute parkrun, given that the next day I'd be going for a sub-25 on Snetterton racetrack.

frost crunch
the Antarctic marathon
entices you

busman's holiday
window steam
by hot tea

At Snetterton, I struggled due to the previous day's exploits at Mulbarton but managed to run 25:54, to make it back to back 25 minute times in the weekend. My poetry friend, Elisabeth Sennitt-Clough, managed a fine 20 minute run to finish first in her age category.

chequered flag
fastest poet
for age

the pits
exhaustion
overtakes me

13. CHELMSFORD CENTRAL

After the euphoria and exhaustion of back to back 25 minute parkruns the weekend before, I visited Chelmsford with my son, just near enough to Tiptree that he could be back for football practice at 10! It's one of the largest parkruns in the country, with over 700 people completing it when we ran. The course takes you under the impressive viaduct through Central Park, winding along the river, through an underpass, over a bridge (single file only) and then lapping around a playing field which has a slight uphill section. It's a straight out and back, and all the better for it. Watch out for the phantom shortcut taker, who rather foolishly uploaded their crime onto Strava for us all to see!

start line...
a runner's sombrero
collecting drizzle

serious runner
not a funny bone
in their body

shortcut
the running watch
never lies

14. THETFORD

Located in Breckland, Thetford is an interesting course with fine views of the ruined Abbey and the river. It's laps of various meadows, but it's fairly flat and off-road in places. The motorbike restrictors do require single file passage so that can slow the pb chaser down. I ran this on pacer week and was grateful to the 25 minute runner, Andy Fleet, for guiding me to a new pb (25:20). It was also Groundhog Day in the USA, reflected by the circuitous nature of the course! There was snowfall as I crossed into the finish funnel, which would have been a magical experience if I wasn't so damned exhausted!

Groundhog Day
the pacer's shadow
bang on time

another
great escape
runners caught up
in a motorbike
restrictor

15. COLCHESTER CASTLE

This parkrun, near to where I live, felt like facing Vader. Its hilly nature was a challenge that eventually I had to face. But only when fully ready. In the end, it was a highly enjoyable experience and those loops around the Castle are breath-taking. Despite the uphill section, which you have to run two and a half times, the tarmac surface makes it possible to boom downhill and gain some of the time lost on the uphill. The Castle itself has a rich history, and was built by the Normans on the site of a Roman temple sacked by Boudica's Iceni tribe in 60 or 61 AD. The Castle housed a notorious prison.

Run Report: The Poetry Dungeon – parkrun #347

I returned to Castle Park with my son Joseph, a little nervous about how he'd handle the hill. It was his 21st different event so I needn't have worried. A critical mass of 308 parkrunners assembled despite the drizzly, overcast weather. Colchester Castle seemed like the typical 'flash' parkrun with hardly anyone around at 8:45, only for an influx of athletes to digest Meera's run briefing 10 minutes later. I should have heeded her warning about the slippery nature of the paths...

Usually, my son and me couldn't pace a corridor, but this morning we were quite sedate in the first mile, enjoying the relative comfort of the first downhill section. All seemed good in the world of Corner Cutter Gardiner and son. Approaching the turnaround with genuine hope, it was dashed as I skidded on some wet leaves and onto the damp grass, slide tackle style. The concern and encouragement of my fellow parkrunners (not my son I might add!) got me underway again, but the momentum had been lost. Streaked with dirt, I hauled my frame up the hill for the initial lung buster in the style of the Marshmallow Man.

Near the café, a lovely marshal quipped 'oh, a poet!' pleased that one had been released from their straitjacket! The best thing about the parkrun is passing around the Castle, before enjoying a well-earned downhill sprint. The hill on the second lap felt like the north face of the Eiger; cheered on by some of the 35 fabulous volunteers who made the parkrun possible. Soundly beaten in the sprint finish by my son, I was left to roll into the finish funnel in around 27 minutes, my stomach muscles aching like John Hurt's in Alien. Interestingly, Sigourney Weaver's mum, Elizabeth Inglis, was born in Colchester in 1913 before moving to Hollywood in the 1930s and starring in Alfred Hitchcock's adaptation of The Thirty-Nine Steps. Herein lies the Hitchcock link to my previous run reports for Maldon Prom (#327) and Newark (#335) which had references to the famous movie director (my favourite)!

A total of 139 runners 'beat the poet' this morning, the wordsmith waning after the tumble. There were over 30 pbs, 13 lucky first-timers (including the wintry Lewis Snowball) and Darren Manners joined the 50 Club. Well done to all parkrun achievers!

We now enter the artistic portion of the run report. On my last visit to Castle Park, I had some haiku poems featured in the report, with the run director suggesting the creation of a Poetry Corner. I feel a Poetry Dungeon is more appropriate given the historic location and infamy of Colchester Castle's prison! The Dungeon should be the home for good, bad and downright ugly poetry. So here is the first effort and a game for poetic parkrunners. It's something called a renga; a sequence of three and two line poems, each linking to the one before, and then shifting to a different subject.

castle hill
now I know what
made Boudica mad

running Romans
charge as a turtle-shell

downhill sprint
runners shimmy
through the gate

marshmallow man
his cadence needs work

breath back
oh look
a castle and snowdrops

And so the sequence has been started by Joseph (2 and 4) and me (1, 3 and 5), with others free to add alternate three and two line haiku poems (forget the syllables!) in future.

16. CLACTON SEAFRONT

Three laps of the seafront promenade, including a steepish slope up the cliff. The third time is particularly exhausting. I ran this on a cold and windy spring morning in 2019, it was bleak and desolate. The week before I ran, they had many runners in orange vests as a mark of respect for Keith Flint, parkrunner and lead singer of the Prodigy who had recently passed away.

orange vests...
for the wind's silence
a marshal claps

tourist
there's no run
like home

17. SOUTH WOODHAM FERRERS

The route to the Essex coast began with a flat tyre in Manningtree. I managed to inflate the tyre with my son's football pump to give us enough air to get up the hill to the garage with the air machine. Managing to get enough air in to reach Kelvedon, I stopped to reinflate the tyre, giving us enough inflation to reach South Woodham Ferrers! During the run, the slow puncture did its worst, and I ended up using my son's football pump, to give us enough air to reach the nearest tyre place.

The course is a one lap route along the seawall flood defences around Marsh Farm Country Park. The views of the mudflats and salt marsh creeks are truly spectacular. The seawall is also home to some rare bumblebees in the summer, which take advantage of the flowers on offer to gain energy and pollen. My son pipped me to the funnel on this run.

flat tyre...
pumped up peewits
make the start

old seawall
you breach
my defences

18. CLARE CASTLE

A Suffolk parkrun not to be missed in the shadow of the 11th century ruins of Clare Castle. Fortunately, the parkrun doesn't take you up the steep path to the summit of the motte, but this is a must run Strava section post-run! The views from the top are panoramic, and I had a good chat with an old man about all things Japanese. I'm not sure how that conversation got started, but start it did, and he revealed his love for Japan. The Country Park also has a disused railway line and station, the former you run along, the latter has a charming post-run café.

puffing along
the disused railway line -
first timers

Haibun: The Seventh Samurai

By the castle ruins on the high motte, you mention the samurai sword purchased on eBay. It's genuine 16th century, from a notable Genji clan. The blade is short, for indoor use and close range combat, we speculate about the height of the warrior who wielded this weapon. I mention the mask of Lord Masamune, a famous samurai from Sendai. Apparently, it was the inspiration for Darth Vader's mask.

duelling…
brimstone butterflies
on wooded slopes

19. GREAT DUNMOW

For me, this was a return to the old days. About ten years ago, I was involved with a river restoration scheme along the Chelmer as part of my conservation work at the Environment Agency. Sadly, the rare white-clawed crayfish that may have benefited from the in-channel berms, are long gone, but the river still has a nice meandering profile here. The parkrun has a riverside section, and is a pleasant off-road ramble through grassy fields, with a deceptively long uphill slope at the end. I nearly went wrong at one field entrance with no marshal, so please study the course route well and keep up with the runners in front!

running river
a crayfish claws its way
into contention

runners flood
over the line
dry river

20. HACKNEY MARSHES

My first visit to Hackney Marshes in ten years, saw me run another 25 minute time on a lightning quick out and back course all on surfaced paths. Last time I visited, a colleague and me were looking for a rare bush-cricket that has been recorded at the Marshes. We also found it on the Essex side of the Lea on the same day, so it had made the short hop across the river. A new insect for the county.

I took the chance to have a look around the nearby Olympic Park, which was coloured by cowslips and nodding snake's head fritillaries. It also provides a chance for a runner to feel the Olympic spirit that was missing earlier on in the parkrun!

Mare Street
late for the parkrun
the hangover kicks in

bare feet
the hammer goes down
on a stone

recovery time
an Olympic breakfast
without onion rings

21. IPSWICH

Another parkrun I'd been putting off due to the hilly nature of the winter course in Christchurch Park. The hill at the start is well known to me after running with my son in a race earlier in 2019. Once up the slope, the course takes you through the arboretum trees, before snaking gently downhill to pass the Tudor Christchurch Manor, and begin the second lap. The Ipswich parks are well populated by ancient trees, including many veteran oaks. It's worth lingering after the parkrun if you have time, to explore the parkland and the Manor.

thank god –
you only
summit twice

knotted oak –
ashes scattered around
giant roots

22. HIGHWOODS

Another newly established parkrun, Highwoods in Essex has to be one of the most picturesque and hardest courses in the east. At the top of the aptly named Heartbreak Hill, a vista of Colchester is afforded, not that you'll have much time to enjoy it during the parkrun. Highwoods has three hills, one smallish one just after the start, and then the double whammy in the run up to the finish. I heard a nightingale on my visit, and woodpeckers are well known from the woods along the route.

not noticing
how far I've come
blind finish

the laugh
of a yaffle bird...
on heartbreak hill
the early pace
just a memory

final hill
the undulating song
of a nightingale

Haibun:

Heartbreak Hill

Saharan dust obscures a scarlet sun, casting an ethereal light on the hillside. It's a strange start to our run alongside the slow-flowing brook choked with silt. As the pace quickens, I'm soon shuffled to the back of the pack, puffing hard, sweat dripping from my forehead. I watch you pull away, until you're lost from sight over the brow of the hill. Demoralised, my legs start to tire and I lose enthusiasm for the chase.

end of the run
my heart rate
increases

23. LITTLEPORT

For Star Wars Day (May 4th) 2019 I travelled to my first fenland parkrun at Littleport near Ely in Cambridgeshire. The first sight of the imperious spire of Ely Cathedral, with a background of thunder clouds is one I'll never forget. The parkrun exemplifies the community spirit of the Fens, the highlight of my visit, a remote controlled R2D2 and a young man dressed as a Tie-fighter. Sadly, the former couldn't go off-road, so didn't attempt the full course, while the wind destroyed the latter halfway through the first lap. Littleport also has its own drove track and mini-fen.

May the Fourth

in the sprint
my Achilles heel
strikes me down-
the circle is now complete
around the meadow

Tanka-prose:

The Sky, Taken Away From Us

I'd forgotten the landscape of The Fens, its large open fields with little tree cover, intersected by drainage ditches. It's a landscape of panoramic skies and straight roads, with few hills or woodland.

at first glance
its gothic towers
remind me
of Dracula's Castle
on a lonely hillock

I can't keep my eyes off the cathedral. The Ship of the Fens disappears from view on the bypass, only to materialise in the distance as I turn the corner of a remote lane and park on the verge. The footpath fingerpost points across a blackened wheat field, which once resounded with the songs of grasshoppers.

cloud shadows
on the old drove
come and go
like hailstones
in spring

The heavy shower moves away on a strong breeze. Several anvil clouds are stacked up on the horizon. The walk is necessarily short; I make it back to the car and turn on the radio, while the windscreen is hammered by rain.

wondering when
the storm will end
the melancholy
of a post-punk band
seems appropriate

24. BILLERICAY

With the words of Ian Dury and the Blockheads ringing in my ears, I pulled into the car park. The route is four laps around Lake Meadows, with a slight uphill section at the end of the lap. Billericay is twinned with Barry Island parkrun due to the sitcom, Gavin and Stacey, being set in both locations. The sign pointing the way to Barry Island is a nice touch, although I can't help feeling that a cardboard cut-out of Ian Dury, whose hit 'Billericay Dickie' couldn't be more relevant. I suggested it to the run director so one day we may see a tribute to the south Essex antagonist.

> ginkgo tree
> and dawn redwood...
> the park lives long
> in the memory
> of runners

25. SLOUGHBOTTOM

Run Report: Run Replacement Service #2

The second parkrun at Sloughbottom Park (pronounced locally as Slow-bottom!) was well attended with 186 people running, jogging, and walking the hallowed 3.1 miles; up from 175 at the inaugural event. The first week's route was obstructed by surfacing works on the Marriott's Way, so a new course (3 laps of the park) was devised to ensure the event continued in good spirits.

We had a good array of Norfolk runners and folk from as far away as Nottingham; 147 first-timers in all, with 20 running clubs on show. Unsurprisingly, just 8 runners managed a personal best, but congratulations to them. The first female finisher was Mabel Beckett with an impressive 19 mins 20 secs, while The Man with No Name was the first male finisher in a superb 16 mins 47 secs, the course record for men. The course age-grade record (90.16%) was achieved by Eva Osborne (75-79) who ran an astonishing 28 mins 58 secs. This will be a tough record to beat.

The event was well supported by 23 volunteers. The enthusiasm of these high-vis heroes never ceases to amaze. I must thank Ben Kendall, the Run Director, for inviting me to write this run report.

I love the freedom to explore that running brings, and with it find inspiration for poetry. It's also an escape from life's problems; a chance to focus on the run and the surroundings. To link creativity and running, I tour around different parkrun venues (as the unofficial parkrun poet!) each Saturday (Slough-bottom was my 50th), writing a short poem or two. I'm currently trying to run every parkrun course in East Anglia (Cambs, Norfolk and Suffolk); a feat I'm calling East Ran-glia (35 events)! I'm only 14 parkruns to the good, but well on the way to completing Tour-folk (8/16 events), Suff-ok (5/10), but some way from tucking into the Camb-wich (1/9)! I spoke to several people who were running Sloughbottom to complete all the Norfolk parkruns; congratulations to them on the achievement.

I'll leave you with a couple of haiku (3 line Japanese poems) to mark the event:

engineering work
run replacement service
in operation

VO2 max
the Wensum runs
at a slow pace

26. LOCH NEATON

Run Report: The Loch Neaton Monster #13

The 13th parkrun at Loch Neaton was far from unlucky with a monster turnout of 177 people running, jogging, and walking the hallowed 3.1 miles. This was the second largest attendance and not far off the course record of 186. We had a good array of runners from the Norfolk Gazelles and over 50 personal bests were achieved; congratulations to all. This week, 48 athletes beat the poet, who wandered lonely as a cloud!

The course age-grade record (88.68%) was achieved by Eva Osborne (75-79) who ran an astonishing 29 mins 27 secs. I had the privilege of running with Eva at Sloughbottom last week where she was over the 90% mark; international class! Interestingly, we had Ryan Lingwood running, who finished first in the inaugural Lingwood parkrun!

I love the freedom to explore that running brings, and with it find inspiration for poetry. To link creativity and running, I tour around different parkrun venues (as the unofficial parkrun poet!) each Saturday, writing a short poem or two. I'm currently trying to run every parkrun course in East Anglia (Cambs, Norfolk and Suffolk); a feat I'm calling East Ran-glia (35 events)! I'm only 15 parkruns to the good, but well on the way to completing Tour-folk (9/16 events), Suff-ok (5/10), but some way from tucking into the Camb-wich (1/9)! We now enter the artistic portion of the run report and we're turning Japanese! The pioneering poet of Edo Japan, Matsuo Basho, wrote a famous haiku (3 line poem) which has been translated by Cid Corman:

old pond
frog leaping
splash

Inspired by the frazzling sun and the final sweaty sprint up Beacon Hill, I wrote the following light-hearted haiku inspired by Basho's poem:

small loch
a runner leaps in
wet barcode

The event was well supported by 20 volunteers. The enthusiasm of these high-vis heroes never ceases to amaze and the tail walker's tail is a great touch. I must thank James Wooler, the Run Director, for inviting me to write this run report. For me, it's Loch Neaton no more, but I'll back!

Run Report: The Loch Neaton Monster II #45

I love Loch Neaton. It has the only loch outside of Scotland (dug by Scottish workers in 1875), sadly without a famous monster. Loch Neaton was used for boating and also ice skating when frozen in severe winters. A concrete lined swimming pool was constructed at the end of World War II, but became disused. The parkrun start is on the site of the old pool. The treacherous north face of Ben Neaton must be traversed at the beginning and end of the run before the summit funnel is reached. Oxygen is in short supply at the end of the sprint!

For many this run was the second half of the New Year's Day Double after Swaffham at 9am. The Loch Neaton attendance record of 186 was smashed, 202 people turning up to celebrate the start of a new decade. Tourists came from Huddersfield and Luton, with a posse from Gorleston Cliffs parkrun led by run director Chris Harbord, including 500 Club legend Nick Overy, tailwalker Phil Laurier, 'Batman' Vinny Jones and Bungay Black Dog Ira Smith. All gave a good account of themselves at the far-from-flat Loch Neaton, after the relative pace of Swaffham.

Run director Sarah Dagless delivered an entertaining run brief with milestone announcements: new 50 Club members Jake Gilding, Luke Gilding, Pamela Medlock, Neil Messenger, while Isla Pearson and Madison Ashby entered the Junior 10 Club. All that was missing was a triumphant mic drop at the end by Sarah; perhaps next time! On our laps of the sports field we were accompanied by songs from Donna Summer, Fleetwood Mac and Michael Jackson. It was Hot Stuff, runners were Everywhere and some were trying to Beat It (the course record that is)! I did suggest Born to Run by Springsteen or I Ran (So Far Away) from A Flock of Seagulls, but to no avail.

The first finishers were boyfriend and girlfriend, Sam Garforth (18:29) and Mary P Scott (21:11), both from Warwick University AC. Well done to them for achieving the double of being first finishers at Swaffham and Loch Neaton at the start of the decade. I wonder how many running couples have managed this or maybe it's a parkrun first….A total of 75 runners beat the poet on my Groundhog Day where I recorded the same time (27:16) as my last visit (25 May 2019). There were 23 pbs in the monster crowd, congratulations to all. The enthusiasm and commitment of the 20 volunteers who made the parkrun possible is commendable. The marshals' encouragement for all runners epitomised the true spirit of parkrun.

In a poetic twist on the Al Stewart song, Year of the Cat, 2020 is the Chinese Year of the Rat. This morning's Rat Run was a wonderful way to start the year, with many more parkrun memories to be made in the coming months. I'm thinking of a 5K to Couch (5K2C) course, these weary legs need a rest for a parkrun or two. I asked parkrunners what their aspirations/New Year resolutions were for 2020. Here's those Year of the Rat resolutions:

Andy White: Having achieved the magic sub-25 in 2019, the new goal is to join the 100 Club.

Dave Walton: Recover from injury and volunteer more.

David Wickerson: Reach 50 volunteer credits.

Joseph Gardiner: Join 50 Club and run a sub-25 min parkrun.

Philip Laurier: Join the coveted 500 Club.

Nick Overy: Reach the exclusive 600 run milestone.

The parkrun poet: Join 100 Club and gain Half Cowell (50 different parkruns), run sub-25 min.

Poetry Corner

To follow her Swaffham haiku and make it a New Year's Day Double, this poetry corner features Swedish born poet Caroline Skanne, an award winning writer published across the world. Caroline often writes about animals such as the humble robin and the longitudinal lagomorph, the hare, which has strong connections with Loch Neaton (it has its own hare called Hareton!). She had this one-line haiku published in Akitsu Quarterly, Spring 2018:

a hare's shape
tucked close
to earth

27. BUSHY PARK

The home of parkrun where it all began on October 2nd in 2014. Paul Sinton-Hewitt led 13 disciples on that momentous morning in Bushy Park. And what a fine location it is for a parkrun. My son and me were joined by over 1500 other runners on our pilgrimage on a clear and very warm June morning in 2019. We were impressed as much by the organisational brilliance, as the wildlife. Deer were in abundance, parakeets too around the two mile mark. The stampede at the start, forced us into some long grass, where we hopped over ant hills. This didn't spoil our enjoyment, just our times! But then it's not really about the times, but the journey. We visited nearby Tagg's Island on the Thames after, a place immortalised in a famous painting of Alfred Munnings just after the finish of World War I.

morning sun
can't see the wood
for the runners

the Lord's
of long distance
bush-crickets

lead bike
the free-wheeling song
of a grasshopper

hunting grounds
a quick time
escapes me

no comparison
the veteran oak
good for age

Haibun:

Bottle Party

An emperor dragonfly buzzes the bottles of champagne, eventually landing on the white table cloth. The large blue insect startles us, momentarily halting the festivities before vanishing into the bankside trees. Glasses topped up once more, the conversation begins to flow freely. She always likes to be the centre of attention, recalling her flirtation with an officer returning from the Western Front in gratuitous detail. My male companion talks of his latest art exhibition, things are really taking off for this bright young thing. A few cirrus clouds circulate in the glass sky as our chatter skims the water.

> water-lily
> my thoughts drift
> to another man

Inspired by Tagg's Island, a painting by Alfred Munnings

parkrun

poet

the Lord's
of long distance...
bush-crickets

morning sun...
can't see the wood
for the runners

28. COLDHAM'S COMMON

Run Report: Wherever I Lay My Rain Hat #35

I'm the kind of guy who is always on the road. And the A14 took me to Coldham's Common on the eastern edge of Cambridge. The 35th parkrun was well attended, despite the wet and windy conditions; 281 people ran, jogged, and walked the hallowed 3.1 miles. It was an excellent field of runners, expertly led by an array of pacers. Consequently, 70 personal bests were achieved; congratulations to all. The Poet's Pacer Award goes to the 31 minute pacer, Chris Poultney (30:59), for being nearest to the allotted time. This week, 149 athletes beat the poet (pos. 150, 26:44), who raged against the dying of the light in the last mile!

I love the freedom to explore that running brings, and with it find inspiration for poetry. To link creativity and running, I tour around different parkrun venues (as the unofficial parkrun poet!) each Saturday, writing a short poem or two. I'm currently trying to run every parkrun course in East Anglia (Cambs, Norfolk and Suffolk); a feat I'm calling East Ran-glia (35 events)! I'm only 16 parkruns to the good, but well on the way to completing Tour-folk (9/16 events), Suff-ok (5/10), but some way from tucking into the Camb-which (2/9)!

For the artistic portion of the run report, we're turning Japanese! The pioneering haiku poet of Edo Japan, Matsuo Basho, was a restless soul who travelled 1500 miles (2400 km) in 156 days, mostly on foot; the ultimate parkrun tourist! My visit to Coldham's Common was my 30th different parkrun event, mainly due to a continuous tourist streak of 27 events. Anyone who runs at over 20 different venues achieves entry to the UK Most Events List on the parkrun website and becomes an official tourist. I've driven 1913 miles (3079 km) from my home parkrun in Gorleston so far, my aim is to reach 50 different events in the next year.

I love the distinctive nature of each parkrun venue and the individual moments which can be captured in a short, haiku poem:

down
the rabbit hole
rain

It struck me that Coldham's Common is the perfect setting for a community event like parkrun. I dedicate this haiku to all who run around the meadows each week:

common land
many runners
one goal

29. COLNEY LANE

Run Report: Yo ho ho and a bottle of squash #79

Colney Lane is well-known in the parkrun pirate community. Scurvy souls travel from far and wide to plunder the hills for another C in the pirate challenge (Seven Cs and an Rrrrr). Accompanied by my son, Joe the cabin boy, I set out in search of a seventh C with a crew of 218 parkruneers and a desire to write short haiku poems to distract me from the pain in my remaining leg.

tapping
along the stony lane
a dog's claws

Undeterred by the curse of black spot, we continue our voyage around the ocean of grasses in the meadow, aided in our navigation by 22 glowing volunteers in a golden age of parkrun piracy.

overheard
near the apple tree
a planned mutiny

From the woodland along the path, a voice echoes from deep in the brambles. "Keep going, he's a long way in front of you" the half-crazed man imparts. I can only assume Ben Gunn means Mark Watlow, who's completing his 50th parkrun and is some four minutes ahead of us on the trail.

stockade
fierce fighting
for position

Becalmed by the first ascent of Spyglass Hill, the pirate hoard thins a little. Two boys set adrift from their father, coast on the ebb tide towards the second lap. The famous parkrun pirate, Paul 'Blueshirt' Freyne, is among the chasers at Colney Lane, his 399th different UK event.

dropped watch
the first hint
of treasure

The final jog up Spyglass Hill is greeted by the outstretched and somewhat skeletal hand of a marshal, pointing towards the finish. The funnel marks the spot for us today; it comes into view on the crest of the ridge.

wooden legs
the biscuit cache
decimated

In the end, 122 pirates beat the poet to the hoard of biscuits and squash. After stealing the last custard cream, I decide to make my escape. Joe says there's a chance of a PB next time; but that it's too dangerous to attempt a second run!

parroting
my son finds
his lost jumper

30. THOMAS MILLS

Run Report: Fields of fire #3

In the Big Country song Fields of Fire, Stuart Adamson sang 'Before the teacher and the test / Before the journey and the rest.' With these words in mind, I travelled to Framlingham and Thomas Mills parkrun, for their third event where 126 people ran, jogged, and walked the long and winding course around the high school grounds and local fields. In the third run, Daisy Glover (18:32) and Adam Howlett (18:06) excelled, the latter sprinting off to put himself out of sight on the first lap and set the course record. Despite the hot weather, 22 personal bests were achieved; congratulations to all. Incredibly, Isla Paternoster smashed her PB by 12 minutes. This week, 50 athletes beat the poet (pos. 51, 28:24), a sorry state of affairs for the waning wordsmith.

For this new event, I've decided to pen a run-through of the course. Notable high school attendees (Ed Sheeran and entomologist Kate Wall) and local Baptist, Thomas Mills, inspired some of the course features described below, in addition to the rapid first finishers and Isla.

Starting near the high school buildings, you complete a circuit of the playing field, before turning north to Howlett's Hairpin. Doubling back sharply after the first gap in the hedgerow, you are now on a grassy field edge path with plentiful rabbit holes and uneven terrain. Here your pace will slow for the next mile but you'll be rewarded with a beautiful rural landscape of large trees, fields and in summer, plenty of butterflies such as the common blue. Chasseing through Sheeran's Chicane on the western boundary of the run be careful to avoid twisting an ankle. At this point, cheerful music plays from a marshal's stereo, a welcome interlude as you approach Poet's Corner and abruptly head north past Isla's Oaks in the crop on your right.

Along the northern edge of the route the path drops into Glover's Gully, before the gentle ascent to the Mount Mills plateau begins. Dodging through Kate's Gate (second gap in the hedgerow) you're back on the speedier short grass of the playing field where you'll pass the finish funnel to begin the punishing second lap. Be sure to have plenty in the tank for this, or you'll suffer around the fields of fire! For those who are interested, I've created a few Strava segments for Thomas Mills, including the full parkrun.

And finally, as promised to Alison George of Coldham's Common parkrun, a limerick:

there was a young lady from Fram
who ran and skipped and swam
until she fell on a run
with Mills she was done
and now she sticks to the gym

31. GREAT CORNARD

Run Report: Marginal Gains-borough #283

This week, the run report will be told through the paintings of Thomas Gainsborough, the famous artist born in nearby Sudbury. So let's begin the poetic portrait of Great Cornard parkrun, one of Suffolk's 11 events. Running all of them is a feat I'm calling Suff-ok, which fits within the larger challenge of East Ran-glia (all parkruns in Cambs, Norfolk and Suffolk). A short haiku poem accompanies each painting.

Cornard Wood, near Sudbury, Suffolk

This Gainsborough painting depicts an old woodland near Great Cornard. The landscape is undulating with a church tower in the distance. Thankfully, the parkrun course is on a pancake-flat playing field but there's little shade from trees, which would've been welcome in the heat. My son took to asking a fellow runner if they could pour their fizzy drink over his head!

tail-walker...
the landscape's rolling gait

Cottage Girl with Dog and Pitcher

This portrait shows a rather melancholic girl strolling through the countryside clutching a dog. Unfortunately, she would be even sadder at Cornard as dogs are not allowed, but that didn't stop 131 parkrunners turning up. Despite the solar assault, 10 runners recorded personal bests and 60 athletes beat the poet, including my son, Joseph, who streaked ahead to finish second in the JM10 category behind Joshua Arnold who ran a blistering 25:05.

distant bark...
the pack gets away from us

Mr and Mrs Andrews

One of Gainsborough's most famous paintings is of a newly-wed couple posing under an oak tree. The seemingly happy occasion is offset a little by their stern faces. In previous weeks a plethora of Andrews have run at Great Cornard; the fastest female and male times being by Joanna Andrews (18:49) and Harvey Andrews (20:49) respectively. The only Andrew in run #283 was Andrew Bigg who recorded an excellent time of 22:52.

sweat-soaked selfie...
a cuckoo bee photobombs

The Blue Boy

The parkrun is well supported by Sudbury Joggers. There were several blue vests in evidence today, along with a dozen other running clubs. The visually impaired runner, Guy Barlow, put in a sterling performance helped along by guide, Michael Bradley. I also spotted Jonathan Price at the start, an old friend from our days playing for the Writtle Old Boys' cricket team.

heatwave...
the sky in bloodshot eyes

The Market Cart

One of Gainsborough's final landscape paintings shows a woodman gathering bundles of wood like a close down volunteer collecting up the cones and signs. This week 23 volunteers very kindly gave up their time. The cheerleader with pom poms kept us all motivated as we circumnavigated the grass frying pan. I must lastly thank Annie for letting me write this report. The following Ann Ford (Gainsborough portrait) inspired haiku has been written for the parkrun director and her volunteers.

inspiration...
Ann chose the guitar
we chose the run

32. BRANDON COUNTRY PARK

Run Report: Snakes on a plain #333

In the run briefing, we were told to watch out for adders. The course undulates through the heathy grassland of Brandon Country Park, ideal habitat for snakes in the open areas between the trees. On an overcast morning, 75 athletes completed the beautiful course. Despite the vipers and long hill, 10 personal bests were achieved; congratulations to all. This week, 29 athletes beat the poet (pos. 30, time 27:57), the wordsmith waning on the second assault of the hill. The event was well supported by many fantastic volunteers.

In my quest to run all of the parkruns in East Ran-glia (Cambs, Norfolk and Suffolk), I ticked off my third Breckland parkrun (I'm calling the challenge Breck-fast). I've also run Loch Neaton and Thetford and have to visit Swaffham to complete the set of four Breck-fast parkruns. A discussion after the run about the infamous Brandon hill got me thinking about the hilliest parkrun courses. Using the Jegmar elevation rankings as a reference (https://jegmar.com/stats-hq/fastest-races/parkrun/), Brandon has 147 ft of elevation and is ranked 354 out of 519 listed parkruns, putting it firmly in the hilly bracket. To find out if you are a mountaineer or flat track specialist, the average elevation of the runs you've completed (mine is 80 ft for 27 venues) and average Jegmar ranking for your events (206 for me), will give you a good idea. I'm classing anything over 100 ft elevation as a hilly parkrun, so get your climbing gear out for those ones!

We now enter the artistic portion of the run report. As the unofficial parkrun poet, I tour venues to find inspiration for short haiku poems. Here's a selection of two-line haiku for Brandon Country Park:

viper sting
the hill's venom

unexpected marshal
Baron Boretto

after the bliss
flint mausoleum

by the duck pond
a cricketer drops his pace

walled garden
runner's high released

monkey puzzle
the speed of a sandal-wearer

copper beech
red-faced, I collect my token

The seven poems reflect the course and the park. The gothic mausoleum was built by the owner of Brandon Hall and the arboretum, Edward Bliss. The ghost of Baron Boretto (Edward's nephew) is said to haunt it. My own ancestors were well-respected flint knappers in Brandon in the late 1800s (Southwell family) which underscores my love of Thetford Forest. Walter Southwell was renowned for his knapping speed, but sadly died in mysterious circumstances.

33. FELIXSTOWE

Run Report: Whistle, and I'll run to you #66

Felixstowe had a place in the heart of M.R. James, the famous writer. His ghost story, Oh, Whistle, and I'll Come To You, My Lad, is based in the coastal town, James renaming it Burnstow. In one particular scene on Old Felixstowe's shingle beach, a figure materialises. This passage follows:

Then, in the distance, a bobbing black object appeared; a moment more, and it was a man running, jumping, clambering over the groynes, and every few seconds looking eagerly back….He was, moreover, almost at the end of his strength. On he came; each successive obstacle seemed to cause him more difficulty than the last.

The classic scene seems to go hand in hand with the parkrun which is probably near to the stretch of Old Felixstowe shore James references. The running man in the bleak and grey landscape adequately reflected the conditions for the July parkrun. On an overcast and cool morning, 238 athletes completed the promenade course. In near perfect conditions for running, over 50 personal bests were achieved; congratulations to all. This week, 95 athletes beat the poet (pos. 96, time 26:26) who was perpetually looking over his shoulder for the chasing apparitions! The event was well supported by 24 enthusiastic volunteers.

We now enter the artistic portion of the run report. As the unofficial parkrun poet, I tour venues to find inspiration for short haiku poems. Here's a selection of two-line haiku for Felixstowe parkrun with a ghostly feel:

empty beach hut
a wall lizard checks in

final mile
I give up the ghost

results list
Roger Moore raises an eyebrow

running man
making heavy progress

tail-walker
nervous glance over a shoulder

timekeepers
whistle, and I'll run to you

After summiting many of the East Coast Alps in recent weeks, Felixstowe was fast and flat; ideal for a quick run. The pier peak thankfully bears no comparison to High Woods (279 ft.), Ipswich (155 ft.), Colchester Castle (167 ft.), Brandon (147 ft.) and Colney Lane (135 ft.). Challenging parkrun routes one and all. I usually pace my 9 year old son Joseph, and he responded here by ditching me in the sprint to record his second best parkrun time of 25:57. I highly recommend Felixstowe for anyone looking for a friendly and fast parkrun.

34. SHERINGHAM

Run Report: Wuthering heights #347

cloud busting
the forecast
wrong again

Checking the long range forecast mid-week, it seemed that there would be thunder in our hearts running up THAT hill; fortunately the storms skirted around Sheringham Park on the day. My trip to the Everest of East Ran-glia was a pilgrimage to the top of the local parkrun world, the elevation gain (279 ft.) and maximum altitude (298 ft.) making it the loftiest event in Cambs, Norfolk and Suffolk. Many warn of the terrors of Heartbreak Hill in the final half mile and rightly so. But there is so much to recommend Sheringham, both in the run and by exploration of the park afterwards. I wrote several two-line haiku on my visit and these are scattered throughout the following report, inspired by Kate Bush songs (previous Saturday was The Most Wuthering Heights Day).

wow, wow, wow
between breaths, windmill view

A total of 193 athletes completed the course, gaining a glimpse of the famed steam train as they descended the hill from the start. The train featured in an episode of Dad's Army. Later, I discovered that runners don't like it up-hill! Admiring the view, one woman tripped up on a tree root. Thankfully, she was unhurt from the fall and continued on her merry way soon enough.

dad's army dreamers
puffing along the sandy track

Alan Smith completed his 50th parkrun and earned his t-shirt, well done to him. The start of the run took us through a corridor of rhododendron, sadly not in flower until next spring.

flower of the mountain
rhododendron

Several pooches were scurrying along the paths with their owners, who gained some much-needed assistance on the hills. A buggy was also pushed around the off-road course; I can only imagine the hardship this must have brought the runner.

hounds of love
on short leads

trail run
the man with the child in his buggy

After the downhill first mile, the middle of the course undulates, sapping energy from runners and walkers alike. I made the mistake of starting off too quickly, before fading badly on the hill at the end; consequently, a total of 76 athletes beat the poet (pos. 77, time 29:15) this week.

wuthering legs
the hills go on and on and on

The trials of mid-run were nothing compared to the final mile where the sting in the tail was revealed. Elevation was gained quickly, culminating in the spirit-draining Heartbreak Hill. The real challenge is to keep on running, even if it appears easier to walk! Despite the hilly terrain, there were 13 personal bests, congratulations to all.

this woman's work
her partner leaves on Heartbreak Hill

breathing
summit air in short supply

A brief stroll after the run meant I gained a terrific view of the woodland from the lookout tower, low clouds descending into the high canopy. I also visited the butterfly garden near the finish funnel, a flower-rich meadow with orchids and a kaleidoscope of colour from purple knapweed to yellow hay rattle. Butterflies such as the meadow brown and ringlet flitted around the meadow, along with several bumblebees. The insect hotel was strangely silent, perhaps the bees were out!

king of the mountain
the bumblebee drone soars

An amazing 16 volunteers helped with the event which I highly recommend to anyone wanting a challenging parkrun in the most beautiful setting imaginable. The moment I came out of the trees and gained the panoramic view of the sea and windmill will stay with me for a long time, as will the sight of the steam train in the station.

35. BURY ST. EDMUNDS

Run Report: For whom the pb bell tolls #309

The 309th parkrun at Nowton Park was a special one with a pirate theme for Kelvin Johnson's 250th run. We saw 258 people running, jogging, and walking the hallowed 3.1 miles. There were 29 personal bests achieved; congratulations to all. This week, 118 athletes beat the poet (time 28:21), for whom the bell tolled after a tiring Twilight 10 k the evening before! It was lovely to see an array of running clubs and fancy dress for the high seas. I tried to find an inflatable parrot and had vague notions of fixing this to my shoulder somehow, but gave up on this as a logistical impossibility. Needless to say, a wooden leg was off the cards too....Kelvin was in his finest Jack Sparrow attire along with several salty shipmates. I managed to engage Kelvin in a swashbuckling sprint to the finish, the very essence of parkrun. Run Director Susan Dunne delivered a sodden briefing, akin to the late Rutger Hauer's drenched monologue in Blade Runner - All those personal bests will be lost in time, like barcodes in rain.....Susan imparted a shocking piece of news – the electric livestock fence was to be avoided at all costs. It was Claire Brown's last run as Event Director. She was heartily thanked by all pirates in attendance. I love the freedom to explore that running brings, and with it find inspiration for poetry. To link creativity and running, I tour around different parkrun venues (as the unofficial parkrun poet!) each Saturday, writing a short poem or two. I'm currently trying to run every parkrun course in East Anglia (Cambs, Norfolk and Suffolk); a feat I'm calling East Ran-glia (36 events)! I'm only 23 parkruns to the good, but well on the way to completing Tour-folk (11/16 events), Suff-ok (10/11), but some way from tucking into the Camb-which (2/9)!

We now enter the artistic portion of the run report and we're inspired by the English poet and cleric John Donne (1572 – 1631) who wrote poetry for Sir Robert Drury of nearby Hawstead. Drury even gave him an apartment in his large house in Drury Lane. Donne travelled extensively, fighting alongside the Earl of Essex and Sir Walter Raleigh against the Spanish at Cadiz (1596) and the Azores (1597). These nautical adventures fit the theme of today's piratical run well. His poetic exploits on the return to England are the stuff of legend too. One of Donne's famous poems is For Whom The Bell Tolls. Here I give it a Bury parkrun makeover (with apologies to Donne or any surviving descendants!).

no park is an island,
entire of itself.
each run is a piece of the continent,
a part of the stats.
if a stopwatch be washed away by the rain,
Nowton is the less.
as well as if a run director were.
as well as if a barcode of thine own
or of thine friend's were.
each week's time diminishes me,
for I am involved in Garmin-kind.
therefore, send not to Run Britain
for whom the PB bell tolls,
it tolls for thee.

36. SWAFFHAM

Run Report: Tornados and Tutankhamun #63

For an unassuming town in deepest Norfolk, Swaffham has many claims to fame. Firstly, it was reputedly a favourite of Horatio Nelson. Our pre-parkrun accommodation was The Swan Inn in Hilborough, an 18th century hotel with connections to Nelson, whose father was a rector in the nearby church. A haiku poem came to mind while eating a light snack before the run, inspired by the curious graffiti on the A11 signs which we'd driven past the evening before:

> Thetford oranges
> pick your own
> bed or breakfast

Swaffham was hit by a tornado in 1981 as part of the record-breaking tornado outbreak when 104 touched down across the UK. The tornados on run 63 were Sri Hollema and David Grindrod as first female and male finishers respectively out of 70 athletes. A total of 31 people beat the poet (time 27:11) who was subdued by a long week at Elveden Center Parcs and struggled on the pretzel-shaped course with the infamous Swaffham 'Summit' (a towering 17 feet, run three times!) and switchback.

The famous Egyptologist, Howard Carter, who discovered the tomb of Tutankhamun in 1922, spent much of his childhood in Swaffham. The infamous curse was said to haunt those involved with the opening of the tomb, allegedly accounting for the Cairo demise of Lord Carnavon, financier of the search for King Tut. Applying this to the parkrun, the cursed athlete in 13th position was speedy Sri Hollema. Fortunately, the course curse can be shed the following week when another athlete takes the position. For the Under 11s who've run this course, a brief poem:

the mummy
out of arm's length
a young explorer

As the unofficial parkrun poet, I tour venues to find inspiration for short poems and was accompanied by my son, Joseph, at Swaffham. Here's a poem inspired by his thoughts on the event:

switchback
we pray for clouds
curse the sun

For those who like adventure, running all of the parkruns in Cambs, Norfolk and Suffolk, is known as East Ran-glia (36 events). Within this larger challenge is tucking into Breck-fast; completing all parkruns in Breckland District (Brandon Country Park, Loch Neaton, Swaffham and Thetford). Attending Swaffham means I've ticked off the four events. Completely pointless, but a little fun nonetheless! For those feeling more adventurous, the Ham-string challenge involves running the four events in East Ran-glia including 'ham' (Coldham's Common, Holkham, Sheringham and Swaffham). Good luck on the tourist trail, it's so much fun.

Driving back out of Swaffham, we saw several World War II trucks heading into town for Dad's Army Day. What better way to finish off a visit to Swaffham parkrun. Don't tell him your barcode, Pike!

Run Report: The Breck-fast Club #85

After last year's double of Brundall followed by Catton, my choice for a 2020 New Year's Day Duo lay in the foothills of Breckland: Swaffham (85 ft. elevation gain) then Loch Neaton (115 ft.). I noted with amusement on arriving in Swaffham that Tutankhamun's

Tapas Bar was next to the Rasputin Russian Restaurant! The ancient Egyptian theme is appropriate for the discoverer of King Tut's tomb in 1922 was Howard Carter who spent much of this childhood in Swaffham. As far as I'm aware (happy to be corrected!) the doomed holy man Rasputin never came to Swaffham! However, Rasputin is thought to be East Anglia's first Russian restaurant. And no, I'm not on commission for promoting these places!

The Pretzel-shaped course of Swaffham has runners ascending 'the hill' three times. The view from the summit is limited but it's not a strenuous ascent. No specialist climbing equipment required. The runner must also avoid the dreaded Sarlacc Pit, the sandy hollow known to swallow runners not paying attention to the terrain!

In the sand pit, runners will find a new definition of pain and suffering: a few seconds added onto their time! The Swaffham Sarlacc is not to be confused with the one at Great Notley. There are four parkruns in Breckland: Brandon Country Park, Loch Neaton, Swaffham and Thetford. Completion of all four is a challenge I'm calling Breck-fast!

To mark a glorious start to the new decade, 131 athletes assembled, many for the first instalment of the hallowed New Year's Day double. Milestone-wise, Gareth Thompson joined the 100 Club, congratulations to him. A posse of runners from Gorleston Cliffs was led by legendary run director Chris Harbord, supported by Vice-Admiral, Nick Overy (500 Club). The first finishers had the unique distinction of being boyfriend and girlfriend: Sam Garforth (17:54) and Mary P Scott (20:46). Fourteen runners achieved pbs, an excellent achievement! A total of 51 runners beat the poet (26:24), despite a course pb for the waning writer who paid dearly for a 'fast' start. Volunteers were out n force, 15 to be precise including the appropriately named Speed family (Dexter, Maisie and Paul). The girl with the large foam hand was cheerfully high-fiving runners, great fun.

We Brits are poor at celebrating our own successes so I asked parkrunners what their proudest moments of 2019 were:

Andy Sawyer: New overall pb (25:43) in Christmas Day run at Hartlepool and also achieved his first course pb at Mile End for three years.

Andy White: Broke 25 min barrier in last run of the year (24:55).

Brian Cook: On 23 February at Swaffham he ran his 100th parkrun and was paced to a pb of 21:47.

David Wickerson: Instrumental in bringing parkrun to Swaffham, after a year of working to make it happen.

Joseph Gardiner (9 years old): Ran Swaffham in the summer, joined the Tourist Club (20 different events) and recorded an overall pb of 25:38 at Rutland Water.

Nick Overy: Recorded his 550th parkrun, an incredible achievement (pb 19:16). Nick also ran his 500th parkrun at Gorleston.

Sam Shelley: Sam was run director today, the 50th event that she's volunteered at. Her pb is an impressive 27:38.

The parkrun poet: Wrote 27 run reports and ran 43 different events in 2020. New overall pb of 25:12 at Norwich on Christmas Day.

Poetry Corner

This week's corner features guest poet Caroline Skanne, originally from Sweden, an award winning writer published across the world, specialising in haiku poetry. Caroline has also turned her attention to writing about the countryside. She had this one-line haiku published in Acorn magazine, Spring 2019:

in this small puddle the whole oak

Given the amount of rain we had in 2019, it seems an appropriate poem with which to start the new decade. The legendary Pedlar of Swaffham also discovered his treasure under a great oak tree in an orchard.

37. KING'S LYNN

Run Report: Unknown pleasures #417

A long drive from Gorleston including a blustery Acle Straight, led me to The Walks. My visit formed part of a long tourist streak which had seen me run 36 different events in a row. I'm currently trying to run every parkrun in East Ran-glia (Cambs, Norfolk and Suffolk), focusing on my native Tour-folk (16 events). I also write poetry for parkruns and if allowed, the run report. I'm by no means the quickest poet runner in the east; that accolade belongs to Lynn regular, Elisabeth Sennitt Clough. Lightning Liz ran her first sub-20 parkrun on 3 August at the Lynn; I've yet to dip under 25 mins. She also edits The Fenland Reed, a top-notch poetry journal with a local theme.

Today, we had 405 athletes run, jog or walk The Walks, with over 40 pbs including Sarah Clough (29:25, JW10). A total of 128 people beat the poet (time 25:52), who was clearly suffering from a foray into the Wild West. I'm more accustomed to the east coast isolation of a windy parkrun at Gorleston, but enjoy regular pilgrimages to far-flung parts of the county. One Lynn ran this week (Sally Lynn Hurst), arriving in the Valley of the Kings (finish funnel mounds) in quick time (21:19). I've written a short poem dedicated to Sally Lynn's achievement:

red mount

a mere spectator
to the pilgrim
who runs every summer
under lime leaves
waiting for a dragonfly
to catch her breath
and hastily retreat
through the valley
of the kings

Cheering on the athletes this week was Elisabeth Sennitt Clough. She's written this wonderful poem, which I'm sure most parkrunners identify with:

On Taking the Lamp-post Turn Three Times at King's Lynn Parkrun

When we touch its body:
flesh and galvanized steel.
lightness of breath, denseness of trunk
wider than any hand-span,
The space between each lap:
lay it down like a smooth song.
There's something honest about a mile,
a solid distance to repeat and repeat…
With the thud of a palm,
the metal echoes, run, run, run.

The metal echoes, run, run, run,
with the thud of a palm,
a solid distance to repeat and repeat…
There's something honest about a mile,
lay it down like a smooth song.
The space between each lap
wider than any hand-span.
lightness of breath, denseness of trunk
flesh and galvanized steel.
When we touch its body.

When we touch its body.
The metal echoes, run, run, run:
flesh and galvanized steel.
With the thud of a palm,
lightness of breath, denseness of trunk.
A solid distance to repeat and repeat,
wider than any hand-span,
there's something honest about a mile.
The space between each lap:
lay it down like a smooth song.

I wind this run report up with a tribute to the magnificent Seven Sisters of King's Lynn parkrun this week:

1. Sally Lynn Hurst (first female finisher).
2. Woman in Joy Division t-shirt. Super cool.
3. Pauline Sparrow. Highest female age-grade (84.62%).
4. Sarah Clough. New pb: 29:25.
5. Sophy Tarsey. Most parkruns (342).
6. Helen Sewell. Most volunteer credits (34).
7. Lynnsport Ladybirds. Women's only club with most runners (7).

Run Report: The morning HE came home #429

Once out of the Essex prison, thanks to the stolen security card, I 'borrow' a Nissan Note from a side street to drive back to Norfolk, the county where I was born in Haddiscoe, October 1957. My village may have changed, the highways certainly have. Reading poetry books about the Waveney Valley has fostered a love of three-line haiku poems.

new road
behind the wheel
old thoughts

I have a long journey to mull things over. The prison parkrun was good training for this Halloween event. The last time I power walked as a free man was at Gorleston Cliffs, my home event. Just thinking about the barcode scanning error fills me with rage, sparking a desire for revenge. They won't be expecting a funnel ducker!

the toothy grin
of a jack-o'-lantern
my face, smile-free

Stopping off, I manage to break into a roadside M&S and steal a Halloween mask, plastic scythe and road map. Back on the tarmac I'm totally lost; ten years is a long time to be away and someone has torn out the page I need. Partially sighted due to the poorly fitting hockey mask, I miss the turning for the A143, and eventually end up on the A47 heading toward King's Lynn! Nearing town, it's eerily quiet, except for a menacing piano tune coming from a window above the Carpenters Arms.

old house
ghost of a boy
at the window

Pondering how on earth I've gone wrong, I decide to complete King's Lynn parkrun instead. The dawn is here, I won't be able to make it to Gorleston in time. A field of 285 athletes has assembled, with ghouls and ghosts to celebrate Halloween parkrun style and four first timers. The parkrun has also been swamped with a late season influx of Lynnsport Ladybirds, dotted around the course.

small joys
hiding behind a plane tree
I scare a spaniel

After a lively briefing from run director Bridget, whose witch hat is dislodged by a gust, and the presentation of the Fields in Trust 'Much Loved' award to The Walks, we're underway at nine sharpish. Despite the Rugby World Cup Final, there are plenty of volunteers today, many dressed as ladybirds or witches, a contrast to my austere boiler suit. I say nothing to any of them. Besides, I've not said a word since that Gorleston foul up.

early twinge
just walk like Yul Brynner
they all said

I'm lapped by the first finishers, a large number of club runners and good for age athletes. But this doesn't bother me in the slightest, I have no need to run. In my sights are the newest members of the Junior 10 Club, Frances Ford and Elizabeth Morris-Sampson, and the three runners entering the hallowed 100 Club, Richard Evans, Nick Mackay and Emma Langley.

plastic scythe
I slingshot around
the lamp post

My 16 victims include a ladybird and witch, the sheer relentlessness of the death march claiming their scalps. No words are exchanged in passing; that would be unprofessional. The game of 'five the scythe' is oddly popular on my last lap, Harley Quinn resisting the temptation to whack me with her baseball bat!

the valley
of the kings
I take off my mask

In the finish area, otherwise known as the Valley of the Kings, I narrowly miss a sub 40 time. More inconsolable rage! I don the mask once more. The impressive total of 25 pbs does nothing to quell my anger. Overall, 268 athletes beat the bogeyman (40:28).

runners
don't fear the reaper
snails do

My psychiatrist arrives and shoots me six times with a nerf gun. I fall backwards onto the grass behind the Valley of the Kings. Stabbing pain in my shins hinders an agonising crawl towards the safety of the stingers.

depression
in the wet grass
leaves fill the space

While the run director scans the park, a few Lynnsport volunteers remain with the doctor near the finish funnel in case I return. I watch from a distance, hidden behind the Red Mount. They'll never find me. I'll be back next Halloween....

empty park
after the chase
the silence

Mike 'The Shape' Myers

PS. The above report loosely follows the 'plot' of Halloween, John Carpenter's classic 1978 horror film.

38. HAVERHILL

Run Reports: High plains drifter #77

It was with some trepidation that I rode into the frontier weaving town (population 27,041) on Saturday morning. The place allegedly takes its name from a Danish pirate, Haver, whose name meant he-goat because of his impressive hipster beard. Haver managed to conquer much of England over 1000 years ago and defeated Alfred the Great in battle. No doubt he would have ransacked the parkrun! In modern times, the Spirit of Enterprise greets the intrepid parkrunner; its nickname of the Haverhill Bog Roll perhaps more appropriate.

The isolated habitation is surrounded by rolling arable farmland, with a lofty elevation around 100 m (328 ft.) above sea level. Its location in a dip in the chalk hills of the Newmarket Ridge translates to a little elevation gain on the course (68 ft.); but otherwise it's a fairly flat run around Puddlebrook Playing Fields. Despite this, a woman asked me if runners were afraid of Haverhill, accounting for the low weekly attendances which make it one of the smallest parkruns in the country. I replied "It's what runners know about themselves inside that makes 'em afraid."

With every intention of painting the town red, I had my new 50 t-shirt on. Just before 48 athletes started their run, a man asked me "Maybe you think you're fast enough to keep up with us, huh?" For once I was, only 12 runners beat the poet (time: 26:07).

With that, we were off, cheered on by the city of Haverhill volunteer force (16 strong this week) and my children's book illustrator, local Carl Mynott. We snaked around the course, the corner cutter guards doing their job well, arriving at the lovely sprint finish after three 'ascents' onto the High Plain! Unfortunately, someone had left the car door open and the wrong dogs came home (Carl's dog Dash was not partaking)!

Mingling with the small but dedicated band of runners in the finish area, one asked "I didn't know how far you could go," to which I responded "You still don't." The beauty of parkrun is its brevity. I get bored on long tourism rides across the plains of East Ran-glia, but appreciate the short, sharp burst of activity on parkrun day. There were some excellent times, and five personal bests, congratulations to all. A special mention should be made of Dougie Millard who ran an excellent 26:31; a fast Under 11.

In a beautiful hour of post parkrun reflection, I composed this short free-verse poem with a distinct western feel.

unknown

parting shot
a marshal asks
I never did know
your athlete number

yes, you do……

I disappear
into the distance
summer haze
at my heels

My work was done, I had completed all 11 Suffolk parkruns (Suff-ok) and now have just 3 left to complete Tour-folk (Norfolk). For the solitary reader wondering about the report theme, it's inspired by the Clint Eastwood western 'High Plains Drifter,' from which the quotes are taken! Interestingly, there are two Clint Eastwoods registered on the parkrun website. One has run twice in Australia, the other is The Man With No Runs.

39. MOORS VALLEY

Run Report: Into the valley #197

On a glorious, sunny morning, 650 people ran, jogged, and walked the hallowed 3.1 miles; the third largest parkrun at Moors Valley. Despite it being a forest moon, no fancy dress Ewoks were sighted, although a wonderful runner dressed as a dog was raising money for Children with Cancer UK. In the shade of the totem pole, Glyn Davies and David Pitcaithley, celebrated their 50 Club milestones.

Arthur Conan Doyle's novel set in the New Forest 'The White Company' sprang to mind, with 'The great PB bell of Beaulieu' (the opening line of this classic work) ringing for 95 athletes, congratulations to all! There were an incredible 127 first-timers to Moors Valley, the ranks undoubtedly swelled by those on holiday, including two Good Gymers from Essex: James Taverner and Dr. Ella Jeffries (third female with a rollicking 21:06).

There were plenty of Ewoks (U11s) present; the top male was Max Sievey (25:12), winner of the Wicket Award. My son, Joseph Gardiner, was unable to stay on target and finished second (25:52) out of 11 male U11s. The first female Ewok (out of 7) was the wonderfully named Betsy (Tink) North (25:22), who enjoyed a stonking duel with Eva Winton (25:23) to clinch the Wokling Award. The future of distance running is in safe hands.

In the weekly contest, 218 athletes beat the poet (26:14), the ailing author finding the early pace too much to handle. Twelve runners from Kingston Lacy Running Club had a good morning, joined by a multitude of Lonely Goats and Verwood Runners. It was wonderful to see so many people at Moors Valley, a clear sign of the increasing popularity of the parkrun, my personal favourite out of the 40 different events I've run in the last year.

Meet the mini-marshals

The New Forest is one of the best places in the country for wildlife. Frequent trips to the New Forest have coincided with visits to Moors Valley parkrun. Alongside the high-vis heroes are the crickets singing as runners pass. The top mini-marshals are:

Wood Cricket

This Nationally Scarce insect is a familiar sound of a New Forest summer as anyone who has spent any time walking or cycling will tell you. It's found at Moors Valley so listen out for its distinctive trilling song from the trees when running.

Bog Bush-cricket

Another Nationally Scarce bug found at Moors Valley in Ebblake Bog among the Sundews and Sphagnum Moss. The parkrun route skirts the southern edge of the bog just after the 2 mile switchback. How many parkruns can claim to have two scarce species cheering on the runners?

Roesel's Bush-cricket

As the parkrun winds its way towards the finish funnel around the lake, you will hear the continuous buzzing song of the beautiful Roesel's Bush-cricket. This species is spreading quickly in response to climate change, and will be inspiring runners for many summers to come.

Other prose and poetry has appeared in run reports, including the following haibun and a tribute to one of Moors Valley's stalwarts who sadly passed away.

Haibun: The Pacer

Tick! Tick! The pacer signals from the purple moor-grass by the track. I hare around the turn, another runner overtaken. Tick! Tick! The course undulates through pine and heath, gravel crunching underfoot. After two miles, I step up the pace, a personal best within reach. Tick! Tick! The bush-cricket's call incessant from the wayside. Tick! Tick!

> bell chimes
> a silent sprint
> for the finish

First Female

so many colours
in the rainbow...
drifting between runners
the first female finisher
a most gentle
blue butterfly

For Glenys

40. BLICKLING

Run Report: Don't lose your head! #294

A long drive from Gorleston, including a sun swept Acle Straight, led me to Blickling Hall. My visit formed part of a long tourist streak which has seen me run 39 different events in a row. I have just two more parkruns to perambulate to complete Tour-folk (16 events), having recently finished Suff-ok (11 events). I've also ticked off the National Rushed challenge for NT events in Norfolk (the mountainous Sheringham is the other one).

Today, we had 314 athletes run, jog or walk the route, supported by 21 magnificent volunteers. A total of 112 people beat the poet (time 27:04), who faded like Anne Boleyn's headless ghost. Milestones were many: Dave Thomas, Vince Keen, Emma Lee and Emily Keen all joined the 50 Club, while Felix Pagan, Sally Bardsley and Jen Armstrong completed their 100th runs. A special mention to Jonah Life, the U11 runner who celebrated his 200th run with a quick time of 23:08. He's definitely a runner to watch out for in the future. Mick Liston celebrated his 70th birthday, bringing along tasty cakes for all. Archie Liston recorded 50:00 on crutches and got the biggest cheer at the finish, a top effort. And now, a Blickling parkrun poem:

the great pyramid

look left in Great Wood, she said
there'll be a marshal, he said,
up the hill, through the gate
pass the distant watchtower
turn sharp right -
you've got two chances

first time, I see nothing
between oak and chestnut,
a speckled wood butterfly
flushed from the stony track,
a grasshopper in bracken
taunts me on the downhill charge

second time, I'm prepared
watchtower, check
knobbled oak, check
speckled wood, check
between the trees
there it is……

a pink portaloo

After an unsuccessful effort at spotting the mausoleum pyramid during the run, I decided to do a post parkrun saunter around the butterfly trail. Retracing my steps up the hill and into Great Wood, I found the mausoleum pyramid in a bracken-fringed glade, from where several common green grasshoppers broadcast their ticking courtship songs. This grasshopper is far from abundant in parts of Norfolk despite its name, preferring old grassland that hasn't been ploughed or sprayed, a rare habitat where arable farming predominates. I've heard it singing before at nearby Heydon Hall, a place my father knew well as a boy growing up in Saxthorpe during World War II. He also loved Blickling Hall, with its connections to the tragic Boleyn who may have been born there, plentiful paintings and long library.

I also spotted a small heath butterfly, a UK 'priority' species due to its decline. When running, we sometimes don't realise the wealth of wildlife that can be found alongside the route. The star of the pyramid stage was a common lizard, complete with a luckless grasshopper in its mouth. Traipsing back to the car, I reflected on a fantastic morning. The parkrun is very well organised, the community friendly, and the rolling parkland scenery takes your breath away. I'll be back!

41. GREAT NOTLEY

Run Report: Running up THAT hill! #280

An ancient Japanese proverb says that "He who climbs Mt. Fuji once is a wise man; he who climbs twice is a fool." I feel that way about the Great Notley Hill of Doom, which stands aloft the parkrun like Fuji! Luckily, we only undertake the ascent to the Bird of Freedom once, twice would be foolish. As a running poet, I'm fond of haiku, which is a short form of Japanese poetry (poems usually 3 lines). A haiku poem by the Japanese poet, Kobayashi Issa, sums up the climb to the top of Great Notley's hill:

O snail
climb Mount Fuji
but slowly, slowly

My first parkrun was at Great Notley in 2017, encouraged by a work friend, Annabel Marriott who promptly buried me in a fantastic sprint finish! In the two years since my parkrun debut, I've lost weight (16 kilos) and improved (pb dropping from 35:51 to 25:20). It's not been easy, and the struggle to improve is far from over, but I now enjoy running a little more, visiting 40 different events in a row in the last year.

For any Great Notley regulars fancying a spot of tourism I recommend the undulating Highwoods parkrun in Colchester, or for the more adventurous, Sheringham in Norfolk. The latter is one of the hardest parkruns in the country (a colossal 279 ft.). Both are beautiful 'mountain' runs and Great Notley is perfect training with an elevation gain of 88 ft.

The top mountaineers at today's parkrun were Kevin Keenan (207 Notley runs x 88 ft. = 18216 ft.), equivalent to climbing Kala Patthar (18192 ft.) in the Himalayas, while Guy Scudder (201 Notley runs = 17688 ft.) has summited Mount Kenya (17057 ft.). It'll be interesting to see who conquers Everest first (29029 ft. or 330 Notley parkuns!).

Today, we had 292 athletes run, jog or walk the route, supported by 28 magnificent volunteers. A total of 95 people beat the poet (time 26:48), who faded like the snows of Fuji in spring and was almost consumed by the Sarlacc's sandpit on the second lap! Congratulations to Amy Howard who earned her 10 Club t-shirt. My son Joseph, joined the Most Parkruns Table (UK) by completing his 20th different event, becoming an official tourist.

tired quads
the hill invisible
on strava

You'll hate me for saying it, but next week I'm off to Japan for a haiku conference and will get to run Futakotamagawa parkrun in Tokyo. I also plan to complete a 5 k circuit of the Imperial Palace, a quite incredible place to run with hundreds of people looping around it every day. In the evening, it's a near continuous parade of runners on the pavements, all scurrying past the Palace moats and walls. For anyone visiting Tokyo (perhaps for the rugby world cup or 2020 Olympics), the Imperial Palace circuit is a must; the largest unofficial parkrun in the world!

42. NEWARK

Run Report: Devon knows I'm missing balls now #335

My trip to Newark was a personal one. I worked briefly at the Southwell (Brackenhurst) campus of Nottingham Trent University many years ago and have fond memories of the area. Dad spent family holidays in Newark in the early 1950s, trips he fondly remembers. I visited Newark Castle on Friday afternoon (parkrun eve). A small sign proclaims 'to cover the distance of just one mile, walk eleven times along this ancient pile.' So the parkrun is simply 33 and a bit lengths of Newark Castle! How easy! I also noticed a mysterious black silhouette in a lit tower window, resembling the image of Norman Bates's deceased mother in Alfred Hitchcock's 1960 classic, Psycho; a very tenuous link to my last run report 'Hitchcock Presents' for Maldon Prom.

ruins

clutching
a sepia photo
of Newark Castle
father's memory
of mother
fades-
all that's left for me
are the towers
of Southwell Minster
and Sherwood rain

So with a sense of family nostalgia, I arrived at Sconce and Devon Park on Saturday morning to make some new parkrun memories. It's an interesting place and a key part of the first English Civil War, with the earth fortification built to protect King Charles I in Newark Castle. The parkrun itself makes good use of the park, taking in views of Queen's Sconce, the River Devon and riparian woodland. Last week saw an alternative route run due to the severe flooding which has affected Newark recently and this morning was no different, the lower half of the course underwater. An added 'bonus' for runners was a prize (my Peak District poetry book 'On the Edge') in this week's 'beat the poet' competition for the runner with the highest age category to finish ahead of me.

warm up
my lungs burst
their banks

I noted with interest, that a runner named Dylan Thomas has been a first finisher at Newark. The Swansea poet of the same name is a firm favourite of mine with his theatrical readings of classic poems such as Fern Hill and The Hunchback In The Park. Given the appearance of Dylan Thomas in previous runs at Newark, this report will not go gently into that good night, including strategically placed 3 line haiku poems inspired by the event, the first two with a reference to the great man's work:

Sconce Hill-
a King Charles spaniel
on the sad height

hunchback
in the parkrun-
my shoulders slump

At nine sharp 165 athletes set off, running past the earth hills of Queen's Sconce and the impressive bridge which leads to the ancient monument.

civil war
runners jockey for position
by Queen's Sconce

The quest for a decent time is further hindered by the absence of the Garmin time piece left behind in Gorleston, Norfolk. Members of the nearby Horological Museum in Upton would no doubt be dismayed.

clock museum
unnoticed, how quickly
seconds pass

We then descended, like a misguided pack of wolves, onto a narrow woodland path by the 'in spate' River Devon. The infamous steps of the Stairway to Devon, thrice took us up to the football field, injecting a fun, yet tiring element into the run. Winding around the football field, some of the 19 volunteers for this morning were in evidence, their task even more admirable on a cool and misty autumn day. The positivity of these stoical individuals never ceases to amaze me. Super organised run director, Sharon Ingle, reminded us to stay off the pitch, although we were nearly hit by a couple of wayward balls (hence the title of the report)! And so the circle was complete and lap two began, runners filtering between oak and dogwood.

riverside walk
a kingfisher jogs
along the branch

By now, energy levels were dropping, the steps more of an annoyance the second time, silent thumbs up are all I could muster for the marshals. Descending into the wood for the final time, the early 'pace' had dissipated.

slow run
perch and bream
go with the flow

Geared up for the final skirmish in this most enjoyable trail run, the football field came and went, no errant leather wind bags this time. After a light-hearted ticking off by a runner for living up to my childhood name of 'Corner Cutter Gardiner' I noticed the Queen's Sconce with its faux armament before the finish funnel was reached after the final slope.

mock canon
my sprint fails
to ignite

Today's first finishers were Simon Daniel (18:54) and Liz Fleuty (24:25), not an easy achievement in the wet conditions. Zoe Smith, managed to run the entire parkrun for the first time since breaking her ankle, and Brian Chapman finished well on a prosthetic leg. Ann White joined the 50 Club, well done to her. Fabulous volunteers were young Theo Falla who helped with the finish tokens and top timelord Alan Robinson.

The highest age graded runner to finish ahead of me was Samuel Spencer (a superb 76:41%), who won the signed poetry book as one of the 60 athletes to 'beat the poet.' After a cup of tea and cake, I was off to the Peak District for some fell running at Curbar Edge. Buoyed on by the atmosphere of the gothic stones high above the valley, I took an ill-advised run up 600 ft. to Curbar Gap, before running a mile to the Eagle Stone which is on the front cover of the poetry book won by Samuel. A poetic end to an exhausting day!

descending
into mountain ash
the path ends

43. LINCOLN

Run Report: The Lincoln limp #302

I'm in town again, master's work to be done. And running IS the devil's business. There are no bishops to trip, chairs to smash, or tables to throw around; besides my mate was turned to stone by that angel from the hymn book. The cathedral's life ban on imps spoiled the party, plus I'm not welcome in Grimsby anymore after THAT incident in St. James. So here I am to cause chaos at the parkrun. The 376 assembled athletes have come from as far as Great Yarmouth, Leamington Spa and Northumbria. In attendance is 5k Your Way, Move Against Cancer, a charity encouraging people to get out and active. There are local groups throughout the UK promoting parkrun participation.

Milestones are many: Holly Brewer joins the Junior 10 Club plus Sophie Croft, Samantha Lewis, Philip Rose, Rebecca Wilson and Steve Marshall are new 50 Club members. There's even joy on Gemma Marshall's birthday! The positive vibes from this parkrun are further enhanced by Doris and her friends waving from their nursing home window at the runners. So much happiness on this frosty morning. It's enough to depress this old Lincoln imp.

From the start, I whirl around the bandstand trying to whip up a storm-force gale to make it harder for the athletes. It didn't work at the cathedral, even on still days, and it isn't successful here. These runners are just too fit, the walkers too fast!! The parkrun poet is being paced around the course by the jovial Hannah Butler (26:11, Vegan Runners); the wavering wordsmith struggling in the sub-zero temperatures (114 runners 'beat the poet' this morning). The moustachioed James Betts is having a good time, running for Movember (men's health).

I try and push the fastest Under 11 runner (Oliver Liddell, 22:42), into the stream. But Judith's Corner is well defended by optimistic volunteers (including the redoubtable Judith); their positive exclamations make my ears ache. Like a sniper, I relocate to Sandra's Corner, intending to jump out and scare folk. What a mistake, Sandra's positivity is the perfect defence against evil spirits. Too much encouragement, too many upbeat words, I must move on. The wood is the next chance for serious mischief.

From my lofty oak platform, I throw acorns at the runners. Passing by is speedy octogenarian Betty Stracey (257 parkruns, 44 different venues including Cairns in Australia!), deftly dodging the missiles. I can't even hit the tail walkers, Stacey Skepper and Katie Stark, two of the 30 nauseatingly amazing volunteers that make today's parkrun possible. The oak branch on which I'm perched bends and snaps under my weight. I've grown fat on the hedonism of Grimsby pubs. Cursing the devil's luck, I decide on one last prank at the finish funnel. As the runners come in, I tap the timekeepers on their shoulders to get them to miss the athletes. This will cause chaos for the frustratingly competent run director, Andy Jones. But the timekeepers are far too focused to be distracted from their task. Not so much as a twitch!! Damnation upon damnation!! There's been over 40 personal bests, rubbing my face deeper into the dirt.

While I wait to trip the tail walkers (small pleasures and all that), an angel springs from the bandstand and banishes me from parkrun paradise with a poem:

windfall

just visible
bipolar nebula
a comet's curse

each new dawn
fire on empty eyes
insatiable urge
to run Steep Hill
until sun down

legs now made
from shingle
and stone

The imp banished to eternal hill running with leaden legs, a prize from parkrun poet, Tim Gardiner (a copy of his poetry collection The Flintknapper's Ghost) is handed out to Doris and her friends for their wonderful support of the parkrun, cheerfully waving from the window every Saturday morning. Here's a haiku poem for Doris:

first frost
waving handkerchief
whiter still

Poetry Corner

This week's corner features guest poet Marta Majorka Chocilowska from Poland, an award winning writer published across the world, specialising in haiku poetry. Marta has also turned her attention to writing about running. She had this haiku published in Autumn Moon Haiku Journal, Issue 2.1:

autumn running
my lengthening shadow
still ahead

44. RUTLAND WATER

Run Report: In a rut #203

I promised my son an early Christmas present, Rutland Water giving us both an R for the Pirates Challenge! I'm now a fully-fledged parkrun pirate having run seven Cs (Catton, Chelmsford Central, Clacton Seafront, Clare Castle, Colchester Castle, Coldham's Common and Colney Lane) and the all-important R. On a breezy but mild morning, 245 athletes assembled at this panoramic parkrun in the smallest English county.

The stunning start point for the parkrun is dominated by Normanton Church and its classical architecture. The lonely building, protected from the reservoir by rocks, dominates the runner's imagination. Along the flat and fast route are some of the 26 volunteers which have made this parkrun possible, and a legion of sheep and their slippery excretions on the heights of the dam. The three-line haiku poems that follow are inspired by birds which could be seen during the run and one that wasn't.

cormorant
wings splayed
in dry sunlight

Runners wind past hedgerows and onto the high dam. It's here where the apparent speed of our efforts are laid bare as the eventual first finisher passes on the other side of the path having already sling-shot around the cone at the half-way point. The dam is a barren wasteland for those that have run the first mile too quickly, dotted as it is with precariously placed piles of sheep dung. It's almost like they know how much it annoys us!

carrion crow
we pick the flesh
off this run

The fact that we are near Bugtopia is enough of a distraction for an entomologist like me, my pace inevitably drops with thoughts of a giant stick insect. Stretched out on the homeward leg of the dam in single file like leaf cutter ants, the church is our target.

crested grebe
ducking for the cone
a marshal bobs up

The church takes longer to reach than you might think, but we make it nonetheless despite the resistant breeze. This morning 98 athletes 'beat the poet' (time: 26:05), including my son Joseph who ran an all-time pb of 25:38. Megan Richardson joined the 50 Club, while Emma Herd and Susan Kidd achieved entry to the sought after 100 Club, well done to all. An impressive 25 pbs were recorded, congratulations to all achievers! It's a shame that Mr Rutland, a male osprey introduced to England in 1997, left the reservoir in 2015 and never returned. His migration of 160,000 km puts our efforts in the shade.

young oak
Mr Rutland
Mr Absent

This week, I was in particular awe of the Rutland Nordic Walk-it group, their first finisher Mick Coogan recording a rapid 37:15 with the poles, followed by Heather Sharpe (40:55). As an occasional speed walker myself, I would encourage others to follow in the footsteps (sorry!) of Mick and Heather. It's great exercise as you should be out of breath and it's easier on your knees; an ideal recovery activity if injured! It's also fun reeling in and overtaking a runner at the back of the pack without raising both feet off the ground! Go on, get that bottom wiggling…

Poetry Corner

This week's corner introduces an excellent running book by poet Helen Mort, herself a speedy parkrunner, award winning writer (of poetry and novels) and author of a guide 'Lake District Trail Running' which was published in 2016 by Vertebrate Graphics. Check this out if Whinlatter Forest is your favourite parkrun! We finish on the first half of Helen's poem 'Rain Twice' published in the Poetry Society Review (2018):

Rain in a headtorch

drifts sideways through the beam,
slicks across a lemon moon

and makes the woods a mystery
of dog-scent, winter mulch.

Pre-dawn, when Sharrow Vale
and Psalter Lane lie down to weep

proud as a grandmother
and not your grandmother

but mine – tears that never fall,
caught by the landscape of her face,

tears a lifted hand could wipe away
and so I raise mine to the silver trees

and pause and look and run again
until I run like horizontal rain, run

with just my failing light
and this false gravity.

We hope to return to Rutland, combining it with a trip to nearby Adrenaline Alley, a massive indoor skate park in Corby. Rutland Water is a must-run event, with beautiful views from the start and the sheep-strewn heights of the dam.

45. SHREWSBURY

Run Report: Chasing rainbows #287

It's been quieter since I booted out that darn menace, Ippikin, for not paying his rent on time. He's reduced to collecting the 20 pence toll on Kingsland Bridge these days. I'm also annoyed with Shrewsbury parkrun. Apparently, I was too big to enter last time; finishing a parkrun in just ten steps would shatter the course record. That Baddeley fellow might also be upset to be trumped in such an emphatic fashion. Besides, where do I start? At the back and I'll squash the tail walkers, at the front and that's Shropshire's future county champion flattened. The spirit of inclusivity meant I should've been allowed to trample The Quarry. Well, I'm going to block up the river and spoil their fun this morning! I set off from my two up, two down cave in Wenlock Edge. I pass Ironbridge, but something's missing…

> cooling towers
> falling gracefully
> a bead of sweat

It's hard this speed walking lark. Plus every so often, a hawthorn bush implants itself in a leathery foot, my Nike Air trainers not sufficient for trail walking. It's not long before the Wrekin dominates the skyline. All those years ago, I had to dump the spadeful of dirt (okay, so it was an unrealistically large spade, but that's Shropshire legend for you!) because of that pesky cobbler from Wellington. And thus the Wrekin was formed.

As I get ready to vault the Ercall, a whistling man stops me in my tracks. The tattily dressed chap, complete with top hat, jacket with elbow patches, and curled up boots, asks me where I'm off to. He also notices my inadequate running footwear and offers assistance in the form of an extra-large piece of foam.

giant steps
damn it, I forgot
the insoles

The cobbler talks and talks and talks. I'll be late for the parkrun at this rate. I finally manage to bid him farewell, but I've already missed Simon Meredith's run briefing. From my insanely lofty height (remember how big that spade was for scale), I can make out 37 volunteers, many in high vis jackets. They've started, 415 athletes whirling around The Quarry. Damn that old cobbler!

Arriving at Shrewsbury, I'm too late to take part. The rage and righteous indignation consumes me. I must find some trees to block the river; I'll spoil the party for Liam Rawlings and Bethany Trow, on course to be first finishers. If it wasn't for that meddlesome shoe-mender I'd have won this easily in less than a minute. To quell my petulant anger, the run director finally allows me to participate. A few lusty strides and I've completed the two laps and destroyed the finish funnel, narrowing averting parkrun disaster by missing the barcode scanners.

at the end
of the finish funnel
a rainbow

I'm reminded over tea and Oreos that James Taylor has reached the 100 Club, Harry Marston-Jones completed his 50th run and Aeryn Atkinson entered the Junior 10 Club. Apparently, 184 athletes 'beat the poet' as the scribbler's pace subsided in the last mile. There were 40 pbs including one for Walking at parkrun's Sarah Cook (41:45). Wheelchair athlete Sarah Ward finished strongly (36:28).

On the way home, I jaunt up the Wrekin in three mighty strides and scratch my back on the transmitter. The Wiccans have returned, another Wicker Man ready for immolation.

Ercall jog
I clean parkrun mud
off my shoes

I decide to set a test for the athletes of Shrewsbury. To complete my Wicker Man challenge (because legs will be burning at the end!), they'll have to run up the Wrekin from the car park to the summit trig point in a faster time than their personal best at Shrewsbury. The fastest athlete from today has run the 1.4 mile route (640 ft.) in 16:23 (Peter Stone: pb 20:51), while the parkrun poet managed 25:19 (pb: 26:18). Go on give it a go, the views are fantastic!

Poetry Corner

I hope you like the different style of run report, told using the legendary Wrekin giant who wanted to destroy Shrewsbury and the cobbler who stopped him. Award-winning editor and poet Claire Everett was born in Shropshire and has a love of its rolling landscapes which have appeared in her poems published worldwide. Claire often writes short Japanese poems, such as this wonderful evocation of the Stiperstones:

white-knuckled
on that rocky throne
when the raven clears
the nights from its craw, will I
be lunatic or sage?

The poem could perhaps reflect the madness which afflicts all those who approach running for enjoyment on a Saturday morning! Rare insects such as the bilberry bumblebee are found at the Stiperstones. Well worth a trail run, don't miss the Devil's Chair!

46. LINGWOOD

Run Report: The Terminator loop #43

Listen, and understand. That Terminator is out there, it can't be bargained with, it can't be reasoned with, it doesn't feel pity or remorse or fear, and it absolutely will not stop... EVER, until it reaches the finish funnel…Target identity: T-800. Stephen Balfe. The Lingwood Terminator. Mission objective: Beat target in sprint finish.

Barcode registration. A3911176.
Portal transfer: Complete.
Target location: Lingwood parkrun, Norfolk, England.
Humanoid. Walking. Pace 5.01 km/hr. Probable parkrunner.
Question: I need your cowl, your boots and your water bottle.
Humanoid: Get lost punk, I need one more run for gold obsessive.
Acquire clothes and miscellaneous items.
Booting Garmin GPS system. Wait 10 mins for satellites.
Proceed to parkrun. 7.83 km/hr. ETA: 08:30.
Parkrun located. Small talk required.
New parkrunner: We're not gonna make it, are we? The finish, I mean.
Response: It's in your nature to destroy yourselves.
Scanning for T-800. Target located: Negative.
New runner's briefing. Scan route. Irregular wire loop formation.
Run brief initiated. Run director: James Pallant.
Tourists present: Leeds, Manningtree, Wanstead.
Canine runners. Terminator detection possible. Proceed with caution.
Picking up podcast. With Me Now. Nicola Forwood and Danny Norman. Check it out.
Athlete density: 87 runners.
Milestone achievement: John England: 250 runs. Nadine Heseltine: 300 runs. Celebrations.
Volunteer presence: 15 humanoids.
Run initiation: 09:00. Start pace: 10.05 km/hr. Sunglasses on.
Humanoid, 500 Club: Come with me if you want to live!
Wire loop. Lap 1. Boiler ash surface. Source material: Cantley Sugar Beet Factory.
Volunteer work party: 27 December 2019.
Wire loop. Lap 2. Ash surface stable. Increase pace. 12.45 km/hr.

Marshal: Keep going! You can do it!
Response: I know now why you cry.
Wire loop. Lap 3. Scan athlete field. Target: Not located.
Marshal: Only 1 km to go. You can do it!
Response: No problemo.
First finisher identity (male): Simon Wright, time: 19:56.
First finisher identity (female): Anna Kirkham, time: 21:27.
Timekeepers. Armed. Not dangerous.
Stopwatch time: 27:36.
Barcode scanned.
Beat the poet: 26.
T-800 presence: Negative.
Run director: Get out!
Response: Hasta la vista, Lingwood!

Poetry Corner

It was nice to see Lingwood parkrun in daylight, having previously speed walked it as my alter ego Mike 'The Shape' Myers as part of the Supernatural Scramble on Halloween. It was just as twisty as it seemed in the dark, surely one of the more interesting courses in East Anglia where you have a good sight of the entire field winding its way around the meadow. In keeping with the canine theme of Nadine's 300th run, many with the pacey Pedro, a short haiku poem of mine inspired by a recent parkrun:

morning sun
a retired greyhound
chases the breeze

The most sobering moment in my running exploits came at Maldon Prom parkrun when a whippet casually trotted passed me in the last mile. I was running flat out (or so I thought!) and he didn't even seem to be trying...I finish with a haiku poem applicable to all who rise early on a Saturday for parkrun, from the gifted Italian poet, Maria Laura Valente:

winter dawn
his wristwatch only marks
free hours

Published in Haiku in the Workplace (2017)

47. BROCKENHURST

Run Report: Heel true, glade straight #338

I remember my first visit to the New Forest as a child. From the early glimpse of purple heather, rolling hills, soporific ponies and the underwhelming Rufus Stone, I fell in love. In Minstead churchyard lies the grave of Sir Arthur Conan Doyle, famous author and creator of the fictional super-sleuth Sherlock Holmes. Beneath the stone cross is a Sherlock pipe and the inscription 'STEEL TRUE, BLADE STRAIGHT' reflecting on his knighthood. Conan Doyle also wrote 'The White Company' a book stuffed with adventure and chivalrous knights, which is partially set within the New Forest; Brockenhurst is mentioned several times on the lead character's journey.

After the long drive from Norfolk, I arrived at Stoney Cross Travelodge with a new-found appreciation of Watford post-punk legends, Sad Lovers and Giants, a 5 CD boxset getting me through the tiresome journey. On parkrun morn, a rude awakening by the thunder of traffic from the adjacent A31, jolted me into action. The windscreen ice scraped off, I slid my way along the frozen lanes through gothic mist, roadside heather bushes crusted with frost. Arriving at Wilverley Inclosure, the sharp sunrise was spectacular, repaying an early start. I didn't have time to find the Naked Man, the famous stump of an oak tree just to the north of the Inclosure and not a naturist! The oak is said to have had a gibbet in its pomp, in which highwaymen were left to rot. A 'naked run' is one free from any devices such as running watch and earphones. I've run naked several times and it's an unsettling experience having no idea of the finish time as you pass the timekeepers. It does make the parkrun email later in the day a nice surprise though! Go on, try it!

The undulating parkrun course looked like the kind of trail run which I 'enjoy.' Not particularly quick, but a challenging run with muddy ruts created by forestry vehicles in recent wet weather. We were lucky to be running; over 40 parkruns had been cancelled due to flooding and the overabundance of mud. Run director, Sue Tizard, did a sterling job with her first briefing via megaphone. Tourists came from as far away as Gorleston, Woking and South Africa. There were many milestones among the 239 athletes. New members of the 50 Club were announced: Si Price, Terence Earney and Luke Linney, congratulations to all. An incredible five runners joined the 100 Club: Vivienne Baxter, Paul Kingston-Davies, long-time run director Mick Anglim, Mark Linney and Matt Cafferky. Well done to the famous five! The run wasn't as treacherous underfoot as expected. Consequently, there was a stonking run by first finisher Adam Jundi (17:23), closely followed by lightning 12 year old Jon Pepin (18:10, 81.83% age grade). The female first finisher was Ellie Marie Monks (18:58), the fenced-off Inclosure not able to contain the Southampton AC speedster's pace! An influx of 53 first-timers was a heartening sight, particular mention should be made of Under 11 Duggie Monger (45:10) completing the difficult course with his father, Pete. It's a tough course to pick as your first parkrun, which makes the achievements of every one of the first-timers special. Welcome to the parkrun family and don't ever give up, it will feel hard at times but you'll quickly improve. A total of 109 runners beat the poet this week (26:57), the waning writer struggling with hills unknown in flat old East Anglia.

I would highly recommend Brockenhurst parkrun, even if flatter ones are available, just for the sheer enjoyment of running in the beautiful New Forest. Of the 48 different events I've run, this is in the Top 5 most picturesque along with Blickling, Moors Valley, Rutland Water and Sheringham.

Poetry Corner

And now for something completely different: a flurry of 3-line haiku poems inspired by the wonderful run in Wilverley Inclosure and the New Forest.

New Forest?
nothing wrong
with the old one

loose talk
you say inclosure
I say enclosure

final hill
it looks far worse
than it…oh #@%!

up and down
like a fiddler's elbows
my elbows

downhill sprint
a stream finishes
ahead of me

Others have been similarly inspired to write, this is my 9 year old son Joseph's (himself a parkrunner) short poem about the New Forest:

Shadows

I was walking through a lifeless wood,
that's what I thought anyway,
I listened to birds singing,
and I walked through leaves.
But I could not see the flowers
for the blind man I was.

48. YORK

Run Report: Unicorns dancing on ice #368

After forays into the Midlands, I finally hit the north for a parkrun. I'd previously drifted no further north than Newark or Lincoln for my parkrun fix; but York's a city that's worth the extra miles up the A1. What constitutes 'The North' has always fascinated me; it being a state of mind and culture rather than a strict geographical demarcation. The consensus at York seemed to be anywhere north of Leeds!

It was my first racecourse parkrun, having toyed with the idea of Market Rasen for a while. The Knavesmire is a magnificent venue for a run, you can imagine the thunder of hooves and cheer of the crowd, as you run round the course (approx. 25 furlongs!). It's a course where amateur athletes have run with Olympians such as Jonathan Brownlee and Laura Weightman (female course record holder). On my warm up jog, the Puddle of Broken PB Dreams appeared to have dried up. This joy was quickly offset by the Breeze of Broken PB Dreams which gusted across the exposed racecourse at around 40 mph. The Knavesmire Knobbler which sweeps down from the Pennines is an infamous thwarter of running ambition.

A total of 618 athletes turned up for the 368th York parkrun, with representatives from 64 different running clubs. Many of these were first-timers to the course (105) and parkrun such as the fantastic walking effort by 5 year old Betsy Wilson to finish her first parkrun in 51:02, beating mum Ellie in a sprint finish. The fantastic support of 34 volunteers aided the athletes, eager smiles and encouraging comments more than welcome on a windy morning.

Despite the strong wind there were 86 new pbs; well done all! We were awash with milestones beginning with Joe McDonald joining the Junior 10 Club. The 50 Club had three newcomers: Briony Mawson, Andrew Storr and Sally Shuttleworth. And last but not least, David Barrett stormed into the 100 Club! Congratulations to all runners for staying the course! An unofficial milestone in the form of Catherine Ward's 200th parkrun didn't go unnoticed. That's true dedication to parkrun!

Personally speaking, 270 runners beat the poet (26:38); I was checked by the Knavesmire Knobbler after going out too fast in the first mile. That I ventured into the Sarlacc's sandpit shortly after the start did not help matters. It was equally as treacherous as the infamous Swaffham Sarlacc and the Great Pit of Notley (Essex)! No-one mentioned the Knavesmire Knoll, the small hillock in the southern part of the course. Oxygen was in short supply second time round!

While scoffing a bacon bap after the run, I was informed by run director, Ellie, of the York Ice Trail in the city centre. Forty ice sculptures were dotted around the streets, melting rather too quickly in the February sun. I managed to find Sonic the Hedgerow, Gruffalo (minus a hand which had dropped off) but missed out on the Ewok and Jawa from Star Wars. It's something I'm gonna have to learn to live with. On my return to the racecourse, maybe the Jawa will be lurking around the Sarlacc's sandpit?

Poetry Corner

To fit with the majestic location, this week's poetry corner features poet Jane Lovell, who has won many poetry awards and is widely published and anthologised. To date, Jane has had three poetry pamphlets published. She also has a love of horses and nature which she captures beautifully in this superbly crafted poem, the last line of which captures the emotion that can consume a parkrunner when they enter the finish funnel for the first time.

Godolphin's Stallion

Beneath the sleeping giant, bones white as hazel,
Godolphin's stallion shifts and twists
with the turning of the Earth, the slow creep
of rainfall through the hillside,
crawling, burrowing subterranean life.

Lost in the soil:
the rush of wind against his face;
startled partridges and pheasant airborne
like winged bottles, birds of Phasis ringing the silence
with their fat rusty bells;

deeper still, his master, long since rotted in his satins,
face drawn to a ghastly leer,
reins, a curled rind, grasped by the bones
of his hand.

The gods remain only in the spines of gorse.
Late June, early mornings, some say,
they flinch at the thundering hooves, the salt
and stench of champed grass as the stallion passes,
eyes wild with triumph.

In the stalls (and possibly lame!), a series of my one line poems about parkrun inspired by famous York racehorses, starting off with the winner of The Great Match against Voltigeur (literally a two horse race!) in 1851. It's said that this duel between Yorkshire horses drew over 100,000 people to the Knavesmire. Kudos if you can name the year each horse won without looking it up!

1. Flying Dutchman slowed down by a headwind

2. those second lap blues Die Hard

3. where's that watter tap - Lake Coniston?

4. Vicious Circle lingering thoughts of another lap

5. personal best missed by a second Heartbreak City

6. Invincible Army first-timers smile from ear to ear

49. GT. YARMOUTH NORTH BEACH

Run Report: Quicksand? #1

I was born within half a mile of the start of Great Yarmouth North Beach, which had its inaugural event on 8th February 2020. The location for my 50th different global parkrun was memorable, but not necessarily for the right reasons! The course is a two lapper around the windswept dunes on the beach, just north of Britannia Pier, and adjacent to The Waterways. In summer the marram dunes are home to some pretty scarce insects such as the mottled grasshopper and grayling butterfly. Adders have also been reported here so you have been warned. For reasons of nature protection runners and walkers are advised to keep off the dunes to avoid disturbance and trampling of the sensitive vegetation and wildlife.

The inaugural event was attended by 160 athletes, each blissfully unaware of how hard the following parkrun was going to be. That no runner dipped under 20 minutes and the average run time for the first event was 34:50, tells its own story. My son struggled round, finding the underfoot conditions rather hard going, even pausing to vomit under Britannia Pier! I personally felt like Ian Hendry running along that desolate colliery beach at the end of Get Carter, Michael Caine gaining on me the whole time as I try to stay upright, his jibe of "you couldn't run an egg and spoon race" ringing in my ears!

On a grey winter's day, there is nowhere bleaker than Great Yarmouth's North Denes. There is a special beauty to the isolation though, the wind turbines on Scroby Sands cutting through the stiff breeze. Marram-grass whipping back and forth. The enthusiasm of the volunteers was a real credit to the parkrun and certainly made a difference on the difficult second lap. It may also be the only parkrun in the world to mention the perils of the scratchy sea holly.

Of all the parkruns, the Sarlacc pits of Great Notley, Swaffham and York pale in comparison to Great Yarmouth: in its belly you will find a new definition of pain and suffering as you are slowly digested over 3.1 miles. It's certainly one of the hardest UK runs, scoring a 9 for its Standard Scratch Score (SSS) on the Runbritain website, comparable to the well-known tough courses of Millom (8.5), Whinlatter Forest (8.2) and Woolacombe Dunes (7).

But for all the hardship, the organisers deserve credit for bringing parkrun to the town, and the volunteers were warm and welcoming. It was quite tricky to know which kind of sand to run on, each seemingly no easier than others inspiring me to write the following poem:

The wrong kind of sand

it's just sand, right?
zillions of fine grains
highly mobile
free draining
how hard can it be?

it's just sand, right?
occasional marram
pebbles and shells
strandline debris
how hard can it be?

it's just sand, right?
sarlacc tentacles
around our ankles
a sub thirty pb
how hard can it be?

it's just sand, right?
take the high ground
find paths not taken
by the shore
beware the kraken

it's just sand, right?
watch the holes
don't disturb
an adder's rest
a grayling's egg

it's just sand?

50. CLUMBER PARK

Run Report: Dodging Dennis #340

The impending doom of Storm Dennis meant I needed a good Plan B after Bakewell was sensibly cancelled due to waterlogged ground and fallen trees. My good friend Nick Harpur suggested the National Trust's Clumber Park in Nottinghamshire as an alternative location. Nick's suggestion was a blinder; Clumber Park is an amazing location. If you like lime in your parkrun, the two mile drive along the lime-lined avenue (1,296 trees to be precise), lends athlete arrival a sense of grandeur. Apparently, glow-worms can be seen after dark, lighting up Europe's longest lime avenue in summer.

The parkrun is well organised and convivial, there's even a hut for the volunteers. Central Bark Café is the setting for post-run doggy style drinks and snacks. The course itself is an undulating two lap excursion. The initial stretch passes along a track between trees, before descending through woodland and passing along the edge of a field to the gothic arch of despair (if you went out too fast!). The path then ascends for 40 ft. up a small wooded hill, before a sprint down the other side, where a bell is rung to signal the start of the second lap. The lap bell is a lovely touch and reminded me of the Moors Valley (Dorset) sprint bell.

After Sally Staveley's humorous run briefing, proceedings got underway in light rain, the breeze strengthening a little during the first lap. Mud was abundant on the off-road sections and the hill delivered its sting the second time! As Clumber Park was my 50th different UK parkrun event, I offered a prize to celebrate. A contingent of National Trust runners were present, so it seemed fitting that the NT first finisher Jago Moles (23:02) should win the signed copy of my poetry book 'On the Edge' published by

Brambleby Books in 2017. Personally speaking, 115 runners beat the poet (27:09), but crucially I managed to hold off Nick in the sprint finish. He had car keys in his pocket and was jangling more than the Manchester music scene of the 1980s so I heard him coming!

It was great to see a few walkers, including Philip and Tracey Moore who finished with Nordic walking poles in a highly respectable 48 minutes. More should try walking back to happiness at parkrun. I have and it's great fun trying to beat your personal best while keeping one foot on the ground at all times.

A total of 363 athletes defied Dennis the Menace for the 340th Clumber Park parkrun. The fantastic support of 24 volunteers in unpleasant conditions was appreciated by all. A special thank you to Nigel Dawber, who completed his 100th parkrun as a volunteer. Two runners joined the 50 Club: Gabriela Hernandez Montiel and Amanda Piper, congratulations to them both. Christine Stimpson finished her 200th run, not an official parkrun milestone, but still mightily impressive!

After a tea break, Nick and I went for a four mile walk taking in the gothic chapel, grotto, bridge (under repair) and the Roman temple on the far side of Clumber Water. We highly recommend this post-parkrun exploration if you have time, taking advantage of the free parking to see all that Clumber Park has to offer.

Poetry Corner

My weekend away had a dual purpose. Parkrun was the prime motivation, but a gig by my favourite Manchester band, The Chameleons, in Holmfirth Picturedrome was too hard to resist. Their stark, jangling guitar riffs and nihilistic lyrics evoke the true spirit of post-punk music. The rebellious nature of the Chameleons would have appealed to the legendary outlaw Robin Hood. The Robin Hood Trail runs through Clumber Park, celebrating the association of Sherwood Forest with the green man. And finally, a short poem to inspire you on your Sherwood Forest running or walking adventure:

Robin's Hood

it's hard
to see his face
hidden deep
within the hood
of a tatty fleece

off he runs
jumping the start
sprinting the track-
rain doesn't touch
his ancient watch

by the time
the peloton reaches
ash tree hill
he approaches
snowdrop heights

but the lap bell
doesn't ring
or the marshals clap-
he's quicker than that
much quicker

at the finish
talk is of the storm,
who ran, no one
even mentions
a hooded man

on the log
a green fleece
the only reminder
I wonder if anyone saw
the funnel ducker?

BORDER CROSSINGS

1. FUTAKOTAMAGAWA, JAPAN

Run Report: The journey itself is home! #24

My third trip to Tokyo was to attend the World Haiku Association Conference. Haiku are short (usually 3 lines) Japanese poems inspired by nature. The event organised by eminent writer, Ban'ya Natsuishi, drew together poets from all over the world including Italy, Mongolia, Nepal, and the USA.

In this way, parkrun is much like haiku, bringing tourists from across the world to celebrate running in a friendly community. My first run in Japan was the 5 km circuit around the Imperial Palace, a quite majestic venue with hundreds of people running it every day. In the evening, it's a near continuous parade of runners on the pavements, all looping around the beautiful Palace moats and walls. For anyone visiting Tokyo, the Imperial Palace circuit is a must; the largest unofficial parkrun in the world!

Arriving early at Futakotamagawa, I met many tourists from London and Australia by the flood defence alive with crickets and grasshoppers (including 7-8 cm long-headed locusts, see photo).

bank steps
thank god we run
on the flat path

The location of the park is beside the Tama River, which flows down through the hills near Fussa; along which many rare species of animal and plant can be found.

storm flow
who can outsprint
Tama River

A view of distant Fuji is afforded on a clear day, but the peak can be frustratingly elusive in the rainy autumn season as I discovered with clouds obscuring its majesty. The famous haiku poet of Edo Japan, Matsuo Basho, eluded to that in one of my favourite haiku:

how pleasant
just once not to see
Fuji through mist

The title of this run report is also a famous quote by Basho.

the rumble
of a train above
floodplain stones

Today, we had 147 warriors run, jog or walk the route, supported by 22 magnificent volunteers. A total of 59 people beat the poet (time 26:53), who faded like the snows of Fuji-san in spring.

long grass
runners scatter
green locusts

The most wonderful sight greeted me at the finish funnel, a murmuration of birds, possibly starlings.

murmuration
the beat of my heart
in the funnel

blossom breeze
runners scatter across
the start line

the last snow
on Mount Fuji
parkrun blossoms

big in Japan
marshals discuss
the hilliest course

2. SEVERN BRIDGE, WALES

Run Report: View to a krill #77

I chose Severn Bridge for the unique Leap Day parkrun on 29 February 2020, a majestic location where Roger Moore's Bond would be at home in a final showdown with the bad guys. It was the first parkrun leap run, the next chance will be in 2048. Excited about the prospect of crossing from Wales to England and back again on the legendary Severn Bridge, I checked into the Severn View Travelodge off the M48. In an uncanny coincidence I had room 007; fuel to the fire of an already hyperactive mind! Sadly, I'd forgotten my passport and running watch. Neither mistake was to prove fatal, passport checks were not in operation on the border (Al Stewart wasn't available!) during the run and an iPhone was used for pacing purposes!

Nerves around the arrival of Storm Jorge and the potential closure of the Severn Bridge due to high winds, led to a poor night's sleep. Despite closure of the crossing during the night, it was open in the morning and the historic event was on. Arriving at the tunnel near the start, the mood was convivial reflected by Jonathan Carter's excellent run briefing in which the assembled mob of 181 parkrun enthusiasts was encouraged to cheer for either England or Wales! The Tunnel of Love didn't live up to its reputation with no proposals forthcoming from women as is the tradition on Leap Days, so Jonathan proposed on one knee to Julian Smith asking for his hand in co-event directing. Thankfully, to save Jonathan's blushes, Julian said yes!

Tourists came from places as diverse as Basingstoke, Bushy Park, Glossop and Manningtree in Essex (me!). Ben Whitbread completed his 50th run, while Ross Howells and Graham Taylor joined the 100 Club. There were plenty of tourists, but special mention should be made of Debbie and Paul Moulton joining the Cow (Half Cowell) Club in making Severn Bridge their 50th different event. Also present was top parkrun tourist, Becky Thurtell, completing her 533rd parkrun and 307th different event. Incredible stats and a top time of 25:17 (74:62% age grade) to boot! We had two Jeffers (run/walk method devised by Olympian Jeff Galloway) from Glossop (Gail Jazmik and Kathryn Gray), completing the windy run in respectable times for 10/2 intervals. And finally, it was noted that the average Severn Bridge run time of 29:02 spookily mirrored the Leap Day date!

Of all the events I've run (52), Severn Bridge is my favourite; it even has a siren to start runners off in Wales (Monmouthshire). The rumble of runners shook the suspension bridge cycleway, slightly disconcerting for a newcomer. We soon crossed the River Wye and leapt over the border into England (denoted by flags) on the Wye Bridge (actually separate to the Severn Bridge). Once in England (Gloucestershire), we passed over Beachley Island, with the high tree canopy providing a little respite from the gusting wind. I noticed a rifle range down below indicative of the military use of the Beachley site by the Ministry of Defence. Once you're off the Beachley Viaduct, the run progresses up the infamous Severn Loaf Hill (64 ft.) to the first tower where the bridge is around 150 ft. above the water (c. 50 m). Between the two towers was the turnaround point, expertly staffed by veteran Syd Wheeler, himself an excellent runner for age having completed 100 different parkruns. The route was lined with 19 volunteers, thanks to all of these amazing people.

Upon wheeling around Syd, the full force of Jorge was felt. I struggled back to the crest of the Severn Loaf where I was able to up the pace a little downhill before re-crossing Beachley Viaduct, the Wye Bridge and stumbling back into good old Wales.

The sprint down the heavily wooded slope towards the tunnel funnel was the easiest part of the run. Sweeping into the tunnel to the sound of a Ski Sunday style cow bell, a last ditch sprint takes you past the twinkling lights of the finish sign and the owl painted on the wall! I cannot recommend this event enough to anyone tired of their home run. It's an all-round 10/10 event from the breath-taking views of the River Wye and Severn Estuary across to the M4 Bridge, to the well organised and ultra-friendly nature of the volunteers.

Afterwards, I took the opportunity to visit Chepstow with its beautiful castle. A Welsh pigeon deposited its load on me, while the town was engulfed by rain, hail, sleet and snow in that order! It seems we were lucky to enjoy the parkrun in glorious sunshine. Perhaps the sun shone on the righteous this Leap Day morning for just one hour?

Poetry Corner

The Welsh poet, Harri Webb, famously wrote in his Ode on the Severn Bridge: two lands at last connected / across the waters wide / and all the tolls collected / on the English side. The Tolls long gone, so my own thoughts on the bridge could be summed up, rather appropriately, in a 5-7-5 syllable haiku: just five kilometres / for Severn Bridge parkrunners / five on Beaufort Scale. The astronomically important day led me to write a poem for perhaps the most extreme parkrun location which may be popular with tourists in 2048!

Giant leap for ran-kind

They say stay away
from the inaugural,
this one's a must run

in a crater on the moon.
A zero-g event
walkers, joggers, runners
all content - footprints left
like Armstrong and Aldrin.
We've managed to book
a cheap return flight,
it's an early start, midweek
on low-cost EasyShutt.
On the launch pad
we check our bags,
strictly no barcode, no time
damn! I've left them at home.
We're not that sure
what a good time will be,
by Newton's logic it'll be slow
given the lack of gravity.
A stunning earth selfie
elation on landing
then the disappointment
last minute cancellation!

APPENDICES

APPENDIX I.
UNOFFICIAL CHALLENGES

On my travels, I've devised a few 'unofficial' parkrun challenges. Below each challenge is the badge earned upon completion. Parkruns come and go; challenges will change with them.

1. East Ran-glia (38 events)

To run all parkruns in East Anglia, notably Cambridgeshire, Norfolk and Suffolk.

Within this larger challenge there are the following:

  i. Tour-folk
  - all events in Norfolk complete (17 events)
  ii. Suff-ok
  - all events in Suffolk complete (11 events)
  iii. Camb-which
  - all events in Cambs complete (10 events)
  iv. Breck-fast:
  - all events in Breckland: Brandon Country Park, Loch Neaton, Swaffham, Thetford
  v. Fen Club:
  - run all Fenland parkruns: Boston, Lincoln, Littleport, Manor Field, March, Soham Village Centre, Skegness Boating Lake, Snowden Field

2. Joggin' Hood (12 events)

Become a parkrun outlaw and follow in the footsteps of Robin Hood. Complete all of these events:

1. Bestwood Village – in Sherwood Forest
2. Brighouse – near to Hood's grave at Kirklees Priory
3. Clumber Park – in Sherwood Forest
4. Doncaster – well-known haunt of Robin Hood
5. Forest Rec – nearest parkrun to Nottingham Castle
6. Hillsborough – nearest parkrun to Hood's birthplace at Loxley in Sheffield
7. Lincoln – subject of first recorded Robin Hood song in 1420
8. Newark – Friar Tuck poisoned King John in Newark Castle
9. Pontefract – possibly where Hood died
10. Sherwood Pines – in Sherwood Forest
11. Wollaton Hall – formerly part of Sherwood Forest
12. York – mentioned in early ballad

Run your final event with an item of green clothing in the spirit of the legendary outlaw.

3. Hillionaire (10 events)

All events with hill in the name. Sorted by elevation gain where known from Jegmar list or Strava for Sunny Hill. The total elevation of 1825 ft. (556 m) amounts to a hill the size of Lord's Seat near Whinlatter Pass (1811 ft.) and Pendle Hill (1827 ft.) in the Ribble Valley.

		Elevation gain (ft)
1.	Blackhill	336
2.	Sunny Hill	308
3.	Hilly Fields	253
4.	Ruchill	249
5.	Pomphrey Hill	223
6.	Hillsborough	167
7.	Oak Hill	83
8.	Harcourt Hill	82
9.	Cannon Hill	75
10.	Haverhill	49

4. Gang of For (4 events)

Gang of Four's post-punk classic 'At Home He's A Tourist' provides a chance for an alternative parkrun challenge. There are four parkruns in the UK conveniently beginning with For: Ford, Forest of Dean, Forest Rec and Fort William. Fittingly, to complete the challenge you must tour the north of the land, possibly passing within spitting distance of Leeds, the home of Gang of Four!

5. Double O Severn (3 events)

In the spirit of fictional spy James Bond complete any two parkruns beginning with O and then head for the heights of Severn Bridge for the final showdown a la A View to a Kill. It's my favourite parkrun for its exhilarating views, breath-defying running and the only place in the UK that you can run between two countries (Wales and England).

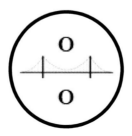

6. Dr. No

Other challenges require the completion of events to obtain the badge. But with this Bond villain challenge, everyone has the Doctor No badge at the start of their parkrunning journey. Upon completing a parkrun where the name begins with the letters No, the badge is lost as the Doctor forbids you to visit events connected to his operations. For example, I lost it when completing Norwich! The badge can be regained by visiting a hospital parkrun. Currently, there are only two (Fulbourn Hospital and Bethlem Royal Hospital) so the badge can only be regained twice!

7. The Wicker Man (1 event, 1 challenge)

To complete The Wicker Man challenge (because legs will be burning at the end!), you must run up the Wrekin in Shropshire, from the car park to the summit trig point in a faster time than your personal best at Shrewsbury parkrun. The fastest athletes from one parkrun had run the 1.4 mile route (640 ft.) in 16:23 (Peter Stone: pb 20:51), while the parkrun poet managed 25:19 (pb: 26:18). Go on give it a go, the views are fantastic!

8. On the Edge (1 event, 1 challenge)

Complete Bakewell parkrun and then run up Curbar Lane to Curbar Gap car park in the afternoon in under 15 mins. It's a 1 mile run but with 600 ft. of elevation it'll get your lungs working and your legs will feel like stodgy Bakewell puddings by the end! Luckily there's a snack van at the summit and the views from Baslow and Curbar Edges are breath-taking. A further add-on is to climb up the Eagle Stone on Baslow Edge. It's not a high rock, but it's devilishly difficult. I've never managed it!

9. The Lincoln Limp (1 event, 1 challenge)

Finish Lincoln parkrun and in the afternoon run up the infamous Steep Hill near Lincoln Cathedral in under 2 mins. It's short, but very steep! Once up, enjoy the views of the Tudor buildings and majestic cathedral.